The Inclusive Leader: Embracing
Diversity for Organizational Excellence

By:
Mustafa A. Nejem

1

The Inclusive Leader:
Embracing Diversity for Organizational Excellence
Copyright © 2024 by Mustafa A. Nejem

Table of Contents

Chapter 1

The Case for Diversity and Inclusion

Understanding the Value of Diversity

In today's globalized world, achieving diversity and inclusion has become a business imperative for success. As the world becomes more interconnected and the workplace more international, organizations must learn to embrace different cultures, backgrounds and ways of thinking to stay competitive. Research shows that companies with diverse leadership and a culture of inclusion consistently outperform less diverse counterparts.

According to a McKinsey & Company study, businesses in the top quartile for gender diversity on executive teams were 25% more likely to have above-average profitability compared to those in the lowest quartile.

The reasons for this financial advantage are clear. A diverse workforce that represents varied life experiences and ways of seeing the world can access more customer insights and make better strategic decisions. When marketing to increasingly diverse customer segments, teams with perspectives from different backgrounds can develop more innovative solutions that resonate across multiple demographics. They are also better attuned to the needs of the heterogeneous stakeholders in their internal and external environments. With diversity comes increased capacity for creativity, problem-solving and an ability to see challenges from multiple viewpoints.

Similarly, ethnic and cultural diversity has been linked to improved financial performance. A diverse leadership team that represents different life experiences and ways of seeing the world can access more customer insights and make better strategic decisions. They are more attuned to the needs of the diverse stakeholders in their internal and external environments.

When employees of all backgrounds feel respected and supported to bring their whole selves to work, it also boosts employee engagement and retention. A sense of belonging is crucial for optimal individual performance and commitment to organizational goals. Diversity enables companies to tap into untapped talent pools and hire the best people for the job regardless of their demographic characteristics. This strengthens organizations with fresh perspectives and ideas that come with a diversity of educational experiences, skills, and backgrounds.

A diverse workforce also strengthens organizations with fresh perspectives and ideas that emerge from the variety of educational experiences, skills, and cultural backgrounds represented within the company. When an inclusive culture allows employees of all identities to bring their authentic selves to work each day, it boosts employee engagement and retention. People want to perform at their best when they feel empowered and supported to do so. In addition, diversity aids companies in accessing untapped talent pools and assembling the strongest possible teams comprised of the best people for each role, regardless of demographic factors. This leads to higher productivity, better decision making, increased competitiveness and ultimately greater success.

Today's global economic reality demands that business leaders proactively cultivate an environment of inclusion where all talents are valued. A diverse workforce should not be regarded as simply politically correct, but rather as a proven core driver of competitive advantage. Organizations that embrace diversity as a key component of business strategy will find greater profitability, innovation and opportunities for growth. The future belongs to companies' adept at valuing and leveraging the diverse identities within their ranks.

To capture these benefits, diversity must be embraced on a foundational level throughout all business functions. As society progresses towards greater equality and representation, customers and clients also increasingly desire to support companies that reflect their own values. Brands seen as champions of inclusion will find favor in the marketplace. Those attuned to the power of diversity will understand it not only as the right thing to do, but the smart thing to do. An inclusive culture where uniqueness is the norm rather than exception equips organizations to succeed today and thrive long into the future.

The value of diversity can no longer be denied or ignored. A workforce representative of gender, sexuality, ethnicity, ability and all other dimensions is a key driver for any enterprise seeking to remain competitive and relevant. For leaders dedicated to building high performing teams, diversity must become an intentional priority rather than assumed attribute. The benefits will be realized through an authentic and sustained commitment to inclusion at all levels. With openness and understanding, plurality can become a competitive differentiator with widespread impact on business results.

How Diversity Drives Innovation

In today's knowledge economy, innovation has become one of the primary factors that determines the success or failure of organizations. The ability to develop new ideas, continuously adapt to disruption, and stay ahead of the competition is essential for survival and growth. However, studies have found that increased diversity and inclusion are two of the strongest drivers of innovation within companies and teams. Exposing individuals to a variety of backgrounds, life experiences, skill sets, and ways of thinking sparks greater creativity.

Research from Harvard Business Review analyzed over 800 new product development teams and found that those with higher diversity generated more innovative solutions and were able to leverage a greater number of perspectives. When different identities come together in an environment where everyone feels safe to share without judgment, greater insights are gained. Novel connections and perspectives emerge from discussions between those with differing vantage points.

Novel connections and perspectives emerge from discussions between those with differing vantage points. For example, an employee with an engineering background may view a problem in a product or process in an analytical, systems-oriented way. Bringing this perspective together with someone from a customer experience role who sees issues from a human, empathetic lens could generate an "a-ha moment" to solve the problem in an innovative new way.

Diverse teams are also less likely to fall victim to "groupthink", where the desire for harmony causes members to conform to one dominant perspective without critically analyzing alternatives. With a variety of backgrounds present, blind spots are reduced as different lived experiences surface new questions and challenges to the status quo. This questioning mindset is a hallmark of high-performing innovators. Greater inclusion leads to more robust debate of bold ideas, increasing the chances of a radical, breakthrough solution being identified and implemented.

When people feel comfortable bringing their whole selves to work, it sparks creativity and autonomy which are prerequisites for innovation. Employees behave more entrepreneurially when they feel safe to freely express their thoughts without fear of judgment or repercussions. This kind of inclusive culture where diversity is seen as a strategic asset is key to cultivating an environment optimized for innovative thinking.

Diverse, inclusive teams have also been shown to be better able to understand customer needs and solve complex problems. With representation from various segments of the population, they can gain valuable insights into the perspectives of multiple customer demographics. This helps ensure the products, services and business models that result from the innovation process will truly meet heterogeneous market demands.

Having a diversity of life experiences and identities fosters an intrinsic understanding of how to approach challenges from different cultural mindsets. Teams are equipped to design with cultural sensitivity, considering variables like language, norms and values that more homogenous groups may overlook. They can test ideas against real-world use cases from a multitude of lenses before releasing solutions - reducing risks and increasing the chances of widespread adoption.

Overall, research confirms that exposure to diverse thinking is crucially important for stimulating the "aha moments" that lead to disruptive new products, technologies and business models. An inclusive culture where uniqueness is welcomed provides the social safety and cognitive diversity necessary for optimal innovation. As such, leading organizations make diversity a top priority element of their innovation strategies and processes.

In today's market, constant innovation is required to survive and stay ahead of competitors. Diversity has proven to dramatically improve organizations' innovative capabilities by sparking new perspectives, reducing groupthink, and fostering a culture where different ideas can be freely expressed and debated. When companies prioritize inclusion as a way to leverage diversity's strategic benefits, they set themselves up for greater success.

Moving forward, leaders must recognize diversity is not just a peripheral issue, but integral to driving value. Strategies are needed to ensure all employee voices are heard and their unique backgrounds feel embraced. Only by translating an understanding of diversity's power into concrete practices and initiatives will businesses fully unlock innovation. Those who invest in cultivating an environment where all identities and viewpoints are respected and encouraged will gain an unparalleled competitive edge in the form of new technologies, customer insights and business models. An inclusive culture where employees of all identities feel safe, supported and motivated to contribute their best work is key to any organization seeking to continuously transform and stay ahead.

Inclusion Creates a Sense of Belonging

While diversity refers to the variety of identities present within a group, inclusion denotes the act of valuing and leveraging those diverse perspectives to create a greater sense of belonging for all. An inclusive culture ensures that employees of every background feel respected, supported, and empowered to authentically express themselves and contribute their best work. This creates a synergistic dynamic that amplifies individual performance and organizational outcomes.

Research indicates that feeling included and able to bring one's full self to the workplace significantly improves employee engagement, well-being, commitment and productivity. People want to feel appreciated for who they are and perceive opportunities to advance based on merit rather than bias. Inclusion satisfies this fundamental human need to belong. When diversity is embraced through inclusive behaviors that foster connection between individuals, teams can leverage a far greater portion of their talent towards meeting strategic goals. However, inclusion requires.

However, inclusion requires intentional effort. It does not simply happen as a result of diverse representation - an inclusive culture must be carefully cultivated. Leaders play a key role in modeling inclusive behaviors like actively listening to understand different perspectives, encouraging participation from all groups, and calling out microaggressions or insensitive remarks respectfully. When managers demonstrate a commitment to valuing each employee's well-being and unique strengths, it resonates through the entire organization.

Developing a strong sense of psychological safety is also important so that no one feels at risk of negative consequences from sharing ideas or making mistakes. Inclusive policies around flexibility, leave, and accommodations further bolster the message that all identities, backgrounds and life circumstances are equally respected. With these foundational elements in place, employees feel inspired to bring their whole selves to work each day. Trusting relationships form as people connect across perceived differences.

As individuals within diverse groups start to see themselves reflected in their colleagues and leadership, barriers to inclusion begin breaking down. With an authentic culture of belonging, previously underrepresented employees feel motivated and confident to voice thoughtful opinions without fear of reprisal or conforming pressure. This kind of full engagement releases otherwise untapped talents, spurring higher performance across the board.

An inclusive culture where all people feel they belong has numerous benefits for both employees and the organization. For employees, inclusion reduces stress, increases job satisfaction and improves mental and physical well-being. People are motivated to do their best work when they feel valued for who they are. For the organization, inclusion enhances collaboration, creativity and problem-solving. It allows diverse perspectives and talents to emerge and be leveraged to their fullest potential.

Inclusive teams demonstrate stronger commitment to shared goals and hold each other accountable in a spirit of cooperation rather than competition. Instead of focusing on differences, members emphasize building each other up through respect, compassion and community. This fosters resilience during challenges as individuals support one another across perceived divisions that too often pit groups against each other. With inclusion as the foundation, organizations perform at their peak as the sum becomes greater than the parts.

Research shows inclusive cultures significantly outperform exclusion norms in key metrics like productivity, innovation, customer loyalty and financial outcomes. When diversity is welcomed into an environment where all people believe they belong, the rewards are nearly unlimited. For any company seeking to thrive in today's global marketplace, inclusion must be regarded as an imperative rather than an option.

The benefits of diversity can only be fully actualized when an authentic culture of inclusion also exists. Representation alone is not enough - employees of all backgrounds must feel respected, valued and inspired to bring their whole selves to work each day. Leaders play an integral role in setting the tone and establishing processes that foster true belonging across differences. With intention and effort, inclusion can develop into a competitive advantage that drives higher performance through engaged employees who feel secure to innovate, collaborate and challenge one another constructively.

Looking ahead, organizations must move beyond performative gestures towards proactive inclusion strategies focused on developing trust, safety and community. Unconscious biases must be addressed, and leadership held accountable for inclusive behaviors at all levels. With ongoing commitment to cultivating an environment where uniqueness is welcomed, diversity's potential for strengthening the workplace of the future will be fully realized. Employers who view diversity and inclusion not just as responsibilities but strategic necessities will reap rewards in work quality, recruitment and long-term sustainability.

Leading an Authentically Inclusive Culture

Thus far we have explored the considerable business benefits of an inclusive culture that values diversity. However, effectively leading such a culture involves more than just understanding inclusion's theoretical advantages - it demands ongoing practical effort. Leaders play the central role in establishing and reinforcing norms of belonging that unlock diversity's full potential. This section will outline tangible strategies for authentically cultivating an inclusive workplace where all people feel respected, heard and motivated to contribute their perspectives.

To begin, successful inclusion starts from the top with leaders committed to learning and growth. Personal biases, even unconscious ones, can undermine inclusion if not addressed. Leaders must examine their own assumptions and behaviors, seek out perspectives that challenge preconceived notions, and welcome candid feedback with humility. By actively working to expand self-awareness and leading courageous conversations on diversity, the tone is set that learning and doing better are collective priorities.

However, commitment must then be translated into concrete action. Leaders can implement inclusion councils made up of employees from varied backgrounds to inform diversity strategies. Regular company-wide surveys asking about experiences and suggestions help monitor inclusion metrics over time.

Deliberate efforts should also be made to ensure all employee resource groups truly have platform to voice perspectives and partner on initiatives. Leaders participate in discussions to understand challenges faced by underrepresented groups.

Recruitment, retention and promotion practices must be overhauled to mitigate bias. Promoting from within shows a clear path for advancement. Flexible work policies allow people with varied needs to thrive.

Training opens minds to topics like microaggressions, privilege and how to be an active ally. Work is evaluated based on collaboration rather than long hours spent in the office.

Publicly committing to inclusion as a core value and monitoring progress holds leadership accountable. When missteps occur, they are addressed transparently as learning opportunities rather than perfection being expected. An authentic culture develops gradually through dedication to continuous improvement.

Here are some additional strategies leaders can implement:

1. Review and refine meeting protocols to ensure all voices are heard, such as going in a circle for comments or using talking chips. Call on those who don't often speak up.
2. Highlight inclusion successes and share employee stories publicly. Feature diverse representatives in marketing materials.

3. Form accountabilities into performance goals so inclusion becomes an expected part of everyone's roles.
4. Identify champions at all levels who can mentor others and serve as a bridge between groups.
5. Make diversity a standing meeting topic to discuss challenges, not just in special events or trainings.
6. Compensate inclusion efforts appropriately like with bonuses, promotions or public recognition.
7. Adjust bureaucracy or long-standing practices that unintentionally create barriers. Customize processes for various cultures.
8. Conduct climate surveys annually and act on feedback with transparency. Share progress to build trust that issues are taken seriously.
9. Form strategic partnerships with employee networks and outside diversity organizations for new perspectives.

Leading authentically requires diligence, empathy and a willingness to challenge assumptions. Over time, inclusion can become the intrinsic way work gets done.

Leading an authentically inclusive culture is an ongoing journey that requires intentional effort from the top down. Leaders must actively work on expanding their own perspectives while translating a commitment to diversity and belonging into clear actions. The most effective strategies incorporate employee input, hold leadership accountable, compensate for inclusion as part of core responsibilities, and emphasize continual learning and improvement.

Businesses that view diversity, equity and inclusion not just as initiatives but as business imperatives will see them integrated at the deepest levels of hiring practices, decision-making processes and day-to-day operations. An inclusive culture becomes self-sustaining when all groups feel respected, growth is a shared priority across differences, and unique voices are equally valued in driving success. Those who pave the way with compassion and courage lay the groundwork for higher performance through fully engaged talent. Ultimately, authentic, empathetic leadership is critical for any organization seeking to realize diversity's promise through true workplace belonging.

Chapter 2

Understanding Identity and Privilege Measuring Inclusion's Impact

****

Understanding inclusion's importance is the first step, but true accountability requires concrete measurement. Anecdotes and intentions are no substitute for data when diversity investments are scrutinized. Leaders need robust ways to track inclusion efforts and connect measurable outcomes to the bottom line. This establishes inclusion as a business driver rather than just a moral imperative.

Measuring inclusion meaningfully first requires establishing baseline metrics across relevant factors. Employee surveys assess sentiment around belonging, engagement and whether identities feel respected. Demographic analyses of recruitment, retention, promotions and wages uncover potential disparities. Key metrics include representation rates compared to availability in the talent pools companies draw from. Tracking hiring sources shows the effectiveness of recruitment strategies in reaching diverse candidates.

Retention rates disaggregated by demographics help determine if all groups feel supported long-term. Promotion metrics exposed by gender and other attributes signal potential barriers or biases affecting advancement. Comparisons of salary and bonuses uncover pay gaps not otherwise obvious. All this establishes a viewpoint into how inclusive the current culture operates and what gaps need focus. Surveying employees on such issues anonymously allows safer feedback.

Additional important data comes from analyzing voluntary and involuntary turnover. If some groups leave at higher rates, investigation is merited into their experiences. Exit interviews provide potentially candid insights from departing employees. But overall the goal in establishing baselines is gaining a full picture of the present realities to guide improvement strategies and later assess impact over time.

Additional metrics capture inclusion's effects on performance. Turnover rates, productivity, customer service ratings and innovation metrics show how fully utilizing diversity translates financially. Natural experiments like before and after a major inclusion initiative or comparing teams with diverse profiles to those less so can offer compelling connections to key business results. Case studies also profile inclusion successes and failures to discern root causes and maximize learnings across contexts. Customer and client feedback about dealt with representative experience also say how welcoming different identities feel an organization is.

Data practices matter greatly for painting an accurate inclusion picture. Gathering demographics needs careful policy to respect privacy while enabling disaggregation. Anonymity in surveys requires smart technical implementation to prevent deductions. Benchmarking externally and among industry peers shows relative strengths and weaknesses that could inform goal-setting. External reviews by consultants may spot blind spots internal teams have difficulty seeing.

Impact must also consider less tangible yet influential elements. Do different groups feel equally psychologically safe contributing ideas? Are meetings and decisions sufficiently inclusive? Metrics here rely on mixed methods like interviews, observations and discussion analyses. Tracking speaking times in meetings or who tends to dominate could reveal inclusion gaps. Polls before and after diversity trainings gauge attitude shifts. Reviewing recent hires' demographics shows recruiters' and hiring managers' potential biases being addressed.

Non-work factors like how welcomed spouses/partners from varied identities feel at company events hints at subtler inclusion aspects for attention. Assessments of knowledge and resource accessibility check organizational barriers exist. Whether diverse representation exists in leadership, communications and client-facing roles sends important symbolic messages too. The full array of metrics together creates a multi-dimensional view of inclusion from various angles. Gaps exposed can then inform where to target efforts for maximum improve and clearest way to measure progress.

Comprehensive measurement paints a full picture of inclusion's multifaceted effects. Over time, data trends shed light on strategies' effectiveness while guiding continuous improvement. For example, analyzing if hiring and promotion patterns for underrepresented groups change post-recruitment trainings shows if the trainings addressed unintended biases revealed. Comparing employee feedback and representation rates quarter over quarter shows dynamics that merit celebrating or troubleshooting. Benchmarking internally year to year and among industry leaders establishes goals and recognition of progress.

Accountability also strengthens justifications for diversity investments that bolster profitability, reputation and employee well-being. Data may convince remaining skeptics by transforming anecdotes into evidence. Demonstrating returns on inclusion through retention, productivity and customer satisfaction metrics attract more allies and resources. Progress reports keep stakeholders informed of efforts' business relevance beyond social reasons.

Overall, measurement transforms inclusion from a "nice to have" initiative to essential for optimizing the many competitive advantages that come with it.

Types of Inclusion Metrics

Determining the right metrics to measure inclusion progress is crucial for driving meaningful change. A balanced scorecard approach addressing multiple aspects provides the fullest picture. Commonly measured are:

Workforce Diversity and Representation looks at the demographic makeup of employees across levels and departments. New hire and promotion rates for underrepresented groups show efforts to diversify the talent pipeline and remove bias from career progression. Voluntary retention examines experience differences that could indicate barriers.

Demographic analytics provide the baseline from which improvement initiatives can be assessed over time. Understanding where we truly are informs sensible, targeted actions rather than assumptions. Annual reporting holds organizations accountable while internal tracking motivates efforts through visualization of gains.

A second category involves Climate Surveys and Focus Groups. Anonymous surveys measure how included and valued all identity groups feel psychologically and behaviorally. Questions assess fairness perceptions, opportunities to excel and raise concerns without fear. Segregating feedback detects disparities needing remedy, such as bias in certain departments.

Longitudinal survey data coupled with qualitative interviews illustrate evolving views as inclusion policies take effect. The disparity reduction rate shows accelerating progress in building an environment where everyone can authentically contribute their best work. Continuous listening bolsters this by informing real-time adjustments as needs change.

A third metric is Training and Development Tracking. This examines equitable access to career-advancing learning resources. Analyzing registration, completion and program evaluation statistics by demographic helps curb unconscious biases that see some groups overlooked.

Mentorship/sponsorship programs lend additional support. Ensuring representation of varied backgrounds as both mentees and guides strengthens the commitment to mutual understanding across differences. Feedback practices' normalization is also checked for disparities negatively impacting progression.

Supplementing quantitative data, surveys here qualitatively assess career satisfaction and perceived barriers or facilitators. Promotion records evaluate fairness over time, as unfair discrepancies will persist if not consciously addressed. Favoritism towards those socially resembling incumbent leadership risks stifling the full range of perspectives an organization requires to thrive.

A fourth measurement category acknowledges Inclusive Leadership and Decision Making. Assessing the diversity of governing/executive teams and new board member profiles tracks growing acceptance of varied viewpoints shaping strategies.

Participation rates, discussion contributions and consensus building are reviewed in committee operations to check everyone actively engages rather than remaining on the periphery. Introducing 360-degree feedback broadens leaders' perspectives on demonstrated inclusiveness in their own sphere of influence.

A final category looks externally at Community and Customer Perceptions of the organization. Brand and market researchers gauge how inclusion values translate beyond internal operations, through things like marketing, partnerships, and community involvement.

A reputation survey measuring attributes the public associates with the company indicates advancement in being seen as an employer, collaborator and neighbor of choice across demographic groups. It identifies any disconnected perceptions requiring awareness of unconscious biases still influencing external-facing policies.

Product/service usage and satisfaction rates analyzed by customer demographics pinpoint unmet needs or unsatisfactory experiences. Addressing such disparities fosters loyalty among all segments through feeling respected. Partnership diversity sheds light on welcoming-fulness to various stakeholders.

Donation beneficiary profiles reveal the commitment to uplifting underserved communities, not tokenism. Events catering to range of interests build goodwill. Progress surfaces through annual perception reviews assessing strengthened ties cross-culturally both internally and externally over inclusion strategy implementation.

While data collection requires resources, a comprehensive analysis incorporating these categories helps organizations ascertain inclusion blind spots to focus amelioration efforts. Regular reporting to leadership keeps diversity, equity and inclusion priorities at the forefront of strategic planning.

Comparative benchmarking against industry peers through anonymous surveys illuminates excellence as well as opportunities for growth. Aggregating anonymized metrics regionally and globally shows societal progression on the issue.

Most importantly, data must drive action with accountability. Correlating findings with root cause investigations activates understanding for targeted program development. Public transparency promotes continued progress through accountability. Metrics hence evolve as a tool for learning, not judgment—a compass, not punishment.

With patience and community building over time, even challenging disparities unravel. Continual assessment maintains momentum whereas dismissing measurements risks stagnation. An inclusive culture becomes self-sustaining when built on facts and progress clearly enhancing equity, dignity and growth for all.

Overcoming Unconscious Bias

Unexamined biases held below conscious awareness pose a significant barrier to inclusion if left unaddressed. Research reveals everyone holds unconscious preferences favoring those resembling themselves due to normal human tendencies towards familiarity and group affiliation.

This is problematic for equity in that attributes like gender, ethnicity or role often unconsciously sway impressions and judgments, hampering objective assessment of people's competencies and potential. Awareness of these phenomena through education helps sensitize individuals and systems against replicating biases.

Unconscious biases manifest in many contexts. Hiring decisions may be impacted by subtly preferring applicants with backgrounds mirroring existing team members. Performance evaluations could show mild leniency towards those with similarities to supervisors due to affinity biases.

Stereotype activation theory suggests biases emerge from mental associations connecting social groups to certain traits. Merely belonging to a social category activates the stereotype unconsciously ascribed to that group. This cognitive shortcut skews how individuals from stereotyped identities are perceived and treated.

Several robust biases in particular recur frequently. The affinity bias favors individuals similar to oneself as more likable and trustworthy. The similarity-attraction paradigm applies this to both superficial attributes and deeper commonalities.

The implicit association test illuminates' automatic preferences between social categories like gender that people are often unaware exist within their own minds. Even those professing egalitarian values demonstrate measurable implicit biases.

Another is confirmation bias, where preexisting stereotypes predispose one to notice and assign greater weight to information conforming rather than conflicting with expectations. Ambiguity is thus resolved through a biased lens.

A core tenet is biases stemming from majority socialization are especially insidious as their holders face least incentive to examine them or advantage from doing so. In contrast, stigmatized groups learn from an early age to recognize both majority and in-group biases as survival strategies.

Countering biases requires ongoing effort as automatic stereotypes are resistant to temporary reminders. Leaders must demonstrate diligence through action, not platitudes. Regular skill-building workshops help surface implicit associations and develop new mental habits.

Exposure to challenging preconceptions raises awareness of own reasoning fallibility. Intergroup contact theory notes stereotypes weaken through quality interaction highlighting individual complexities over superficial attributes. Identifying exemplars defying expectations also helps broaden perspectives.

Accountability measures recognize not all biases can be expunged, but mindfulness and checks can minimize unfair impacts. Name-blind recruitment and assessment removes identifying details, as can diversifying interview panels.

Rotation across functions exposes assumptive thinking. Inclusive language acknowledges multiple realities, versus asserting a sole dominant narrative. Fair processes addressing even subtle grievances build faith in an organization's justice system over time.

Leaders modeling reflective self-critique encourages others to acknowledge blind spots respectfully. Together, these strategies rewire automatic patterns via education and practice. Rather than accusations, emphasize bias as a normal yet improvable human condition through compassion and community.

Progress stems not from overnight transformation, but steady nurturing of empathy, responsibility and care across differences within systems. Accountability resting also on intentions versus unintended errors assists cooperation instead of defensiveness.

Long term success requires cultivating understanding that prospers from open exchange of all perspectives, not dominance of any single view. With patience and good faith, even entrenched biases relinquish influence through respect and relationship. An inclusive environment emerges where people freely contribute as their full, complex selves. Although challenging, consciously facing biases builds a future advancing fairness for all.

The Impact of Macroaggressions

Subtle forms of discrimination prevalent in social interactions undermine inclusion less visibly than overt acts yet profoundly. termed microaggressions, these everyday verbal, nonverbal or environmental indignities communicate hostile, derogatory slights to marginalized groups.

Though unintentional and often committed unconsciously, accumulated impact upon targets can parallel macro assaults through conveyed invalidation, irritation and fatigue. Perpetrators may not recognize microaggressions' hidden messages or how they affect recipients differently than themselves.

Examples include ascribing a person's success to their race or gender instead of merit. Other common themes are exoticization of cultural display, assumption of criminality due to race and invalidation of intersecting identities.

Microaggressions trigger stress responses like rumination and hypervigilance over time. Targets focus excess energy discerning intended versus unintended offense which distracts from performance and wellbeing. Isolation intensifies as calling out micro assaults risks labels like "oversensitivity."

Some impacts of sustained microaggressions include internalized oppression where targets accept put-downs as deserved. Physical health also associates to chronic perceived discrimination through prolonged fight-or-flight activation.

Mental health issues like depression and anxiety more commonly afflict target groups alongside diminished self-esteem and worldview. Workplace effects involve disengagement, lower job satisfaction and higher turnover.

Those with intersectional identities experience "multipliers" from microaggressions targeting multiple aspects. A black woman faces unique marginalization compared to facing race or sex bias alone. Cumulative stress accumulates quickly at these intersections.

While intentions differ from overt prejudice, impacts matter more to targets than perceived maliciousness behind the act. Well-meaning microaggressions still convey marginalizing outsider status through hidden affronts to dignity.

Subtle bias also more easily denies, downplays and rationalizes vs overt acts. This renders microaggressions among the most insidious obstacles to equity as ill intentions absolve perpetrators of responsibility for harm.

To counter microaggressions, awareness must precede accountability. Perpetrators listen respectfully to understand hidden harms better than intents alone. Targets feel empowered signaling offense without accusers' defensiveness inhibiting learning.

Microaggression training exposes common subtle bias themes. Practicing inclusive language encourages reflecting before speaking versus automatic responses. Assuming best intent means not taking ambiguous slights personally but still addressing impacts.

Accountability measures again focus on impact versus intention. Policies set clear behavioral standards while prioritizing education above punishment. Bias interrupters diffuse tension in the moment by naming the microaggression respectfully.

An organization's responsiveness builds confidence that marginalized voices impact change. While perpetrators may disagree on any one incident, listening establishes good faith to address recurring impacts through an equity lens together over time.

Such an environment fosters bringing all of one's self, and acceptance of others as whole people, to work freely each day. Only thus can microaggressions cease sabotaging inclusion from within systems claiming to cultivate it.

Leaders model commitment to equitable, psychologically safe workplaces by promptly addressing even subtle exclusionary acts. They appreciate microaggressions' cumulative toll through empathetic rather than defensive stances.

Dialogue skills facilitate difficult yet necessary discussions where all parties progress. Focusing on impact and solution, not blame, encourages cooperation. Leaders prioritize targets' wellbeing and experiences over perpetrators' comfort.

Recurring bias trainings sustain awareness as automatic patterns re-emerge without conscious effort. Empowering bystanders through education on interrupting microaggressions respects all staff equally.

Progress requires persistent patience. As with overcoming larger prejudices, dismantling microaggressions happens gradually through community instead of mandates. An inclusive culture emerges as an accessible, caring environment where each person feels respected for bringing their authentic, complete self. With care and commitment, even subtle exclusions relinquish power through relationships of dignity for all.

Chapter 3

Diversity Best Practices in the Workplace

Recruiting and Hiring a Diverse Workforce

Attracting qualified candidates across demographic groups begins by examining recruitment processes for unconscious biases. Postings employ inclusive language describing the job and company positively for diverse pools.

They appear in venues catering to various gender, ethnic, disability and age demographics. Partnerships with organizations assisting underrepresented communities spread awareness. University recruitment targets programs promoting diversity in relevant fields.

Job descriptions focus on required qualifications rather than preferred attributes, allowing varied candidates applying skills equivalently. Assessing accomplishments objectively identifies strengths regardless gender or background.

Anonymized application screening hides identifying data prone to bias triggers like names. Diverse panels review qualifications following structured rating rubrics. Interviews utilize behavioral questions assessing competence irrespective identity.

Standardized scoring calibrates assessments fairly across interviews. Documentation addresses only job-relevant factors to prevent subjective attributes improperly influencing hiring.

Consideration of candidates benefits from factoring systemic barriers faced differentially according to identity. For example, career interruptions for caregiving affect predominately mothers yet resilience is built navigating such adversity.

Fair chance hiring programs acknowledge equity over strict conventions when multiple candidates comparably meet requirements. Targeted internships and trainee roles introduce opportunities for networking into career paths.

Onboarding cultivates inclusion through mentoring, affinity groups and tolerance for various workstyles, needs and identities coexisting respectfully. Surveys assess onboarding experiences to address issues privileging any backgrounds.

Compensation evaluates jobs based on responsibilities, not employee attributes. Benefits accommodate diverse circumstances through health plans catering various requirements and flexible work policies balancing multiple life facets.

These practices establish an inclusive employer brand attractive to exceptional candidates regardless demography through equitable, bias-resistant recruitment enabling talents across identities.

Fastening diversity necessitates continuous refinement. Exit interviews reveal whether any groups perceived unfair treatment by reconsidering only constructive suggestions.

Complaint systems encourage concerns voiced professionally and in good faith. Investigations remain impartial with all parties heard respectfully but disciplines selectively for egregious not ambiguous conduct.

Focusing on impact over intentions builds understanding while accountability targets resolution not blame. Mediation helps conflicting parties find mutually agreeable solutions through open dialogue instead of finger-pointing.

Leaders model accountability through due diligence. They examine failures transparently with specific plans for prevention, not defensiveness. Commitment conveys through allocating diversity resources proportionate to its professed priority.

Metrics measure diversity hiring success holistically over time rather than annual fluctuations. Qualitative appreciation balances quantitative data recognizing not all valued traits correlate strictly to demographics. Continuous progress matters most.

Maintaining diverse groups necessitates retention efforts as hiring alone proves insufficient. Flexible work promotes work-life integration and accessibility for circumstances like disabilities or caregiving demanding accommodation.

Mentorship pairs new hires with sponsor allies enhancing skills, resources and sponsorship for promotions disfavoring some demographics traditionally. Inclusive leadership and management development programs cultivate diverse successors to leadership pipelines still lagging representation.

Compensation reviews address persistent biases like underpaying "women's work" to ensure parity irrespective role or identity. Anti-bias training sustains through refresher sessions addressing issues emerging from changing social contexts and employee turnover.

Surveying employee experiences regularly gauges perceptions of fairness, respect and inclusion qualitatively beyond demographics. Issues are addressed constructively through community-building over defensiveness or isolation.

With persistence and good faith, an organization can establish equitable, welcoming recruitment removing participation barriers to attract and retain diverse talents enhancing its sustainability, resilience and social mission over time. Progress requires commitment to inclusive excellence beyond isolated initiatives.

Retaining Talent from All Backgrounds

Career development opportunities like mentorship and sponsorship correlate strongly to retention especially for women and minorities faced bias. Programs pair new hires with senior sponsors aiding navigation.

Mentorship cultivates inclusion and belonging. Mentees gain support systems reducing isolating tendencies accompanying "outsider" status. Senior sponsors advise on organization norms and politics assisting advancement invisible to outsiders.

Leadership training exposes talents to strategic perspectives and succession planning. It demonstrates commitment to equitable promotion paths regardless gender or race which attrition data may show obstructed traditionally.

Flexible work policies allow telecommuting, adjusted hours, compressed schedules or leaves for circumstances like caregiving disproportionately impacting women and people with disabilities. Work-life balance proves vital to retention.

Recognizing differing needs maintains respect for various identities. Surveys assess inclusion qualitatively to address issues before attrition results from an unwelcoming culture versus compensation alone.

Compensation reviews target known bias risks. Gender and racial pay gaps undermine retention when talents perceive unfair treatment reducible. Inequality surfaces through analyzing equity indexes factoring role, experience, performance and education.

Crowdsourced review sites also reveal biases if disparaging reputations form around any groups. Addressing such issues proactively builds reputations attracting diverse candidates.

Performance management reformed to prevent biases obscuring contributions of talents facing discrimination. Objective sales and productivity metrics apply fairly to evaluate all staff regardless identity or background.

Soft attributes prone to subjectivity like "fit" cannot determine ratings or promotions disfavoring women and minorities showing pretexts often veil biasrisks. Structured assessments ensure equitable treatment.

Exit interviews maintained confidentially determine reasons for attrition to amend deficiencies before diverse talents conclude the environment remains unwelcoming and leave. Continuous improvement sustains retention.

Grievance systems facilitate respectful dialogue on concerns, aiming resolution over discipline. An impartial ombudsperson helps conflicting parties find cooperation-focused, mutually agreeable solutions through open communication instead of accusations.

Anti-harassment and civility training sustains through refresher courses cognizant changing social contexts and new employees. Bystander intervention empowers all staff upholding respect for all. Leadership models accountability through proper handling even ambiguous complaints.

Networking events and affinity groups enhance inclusion. They connect professionals facing shared challenges to build understandings lessening isolation. Informal mentoring expands from such relationships strengthening commitment.

Leadership commits resources and prioritization proportionate to inclusion significance voiced. Targeted internships introduce untapped talent pools into career pipelines through sponsorship. Sponsorship broadens pools accessed for permanent roles afterward as well.

Data transparently measures progress qualitatively and quantitatively, with issues constructively addressed. Continuous improvement through cooperation maintains an inclusive culture indispensable for retention.

Surveying experiences of underrepresented groups regarding respect, psychological safety and equitable treatment acts on issues before high-potential talents conclude bias risks stay unaddressed. Anonymous feedback preserves candor.

Resource groups receive support corresponding to the priority leadership ascribes inclusion publicly. Their value increases through active partnering with senior sponsors assisting networking.

Succession planning broadens to include candidates from nontraditional backgrounds aided by targeted development. This demonstrates an inclusive definition of talent and potential benefiting retention.

Workplace decor and imagery reflects the diversity represented to foster an atmosphere of belonging for all. Inclusive language becomes habit through bias training stressing respect irrespective differences.

Partnerships with community organizations assisting underserved populations introduce fresh talent pipelines. Internships and traineeship placements improve retention through pathways created into careers through sponsorship relationships formed.

Sustained retention requires continuous efforts understanding systemic obstacles correlated with identity remain to be overcome, through cooperation and good faith on all sides. An equitable culture proves itself over the long term through ongoing refinement.

Fostering an Inclusive Culture

An inclusive culture ensures all staff experience equal respect and psychological safety to contribute fully regardless of attributes. Leaders model respect through inclusive language, unbiased decision-making, and accountability addressing even subtle issues.

Networking and affinity groups enhance inclusion through intersections of diverse identity aspects like women of color or LGBTQ+ affinity groups. They connect professionals in supporting communities reducing isolation obstacles.

All voices achieve representation in initiatives through employee resource groups bringing diverse perspectives into strategizing. Two-way communication keeps leadership transparently responsive to concerns while employees understand rationale for decisions.

Awareness training stresses respect irrespective attributes, orienting new hires. Refresher courses address subtler bias manifestations and issues emerging from changing social contexts. Interactive discussions prompt reflection better than passive sessions.

Inclusive leadership assessments and development programs broaden succession pipelines still observed lagging in diversity. Sponsorship pairs high-potentials with senior allies enhancing access to strategic perspectives and resources.

Unbiased performance evaluation structures mitigate biases risking obscuring contributions. Individual development planning sets equitable goals emphasizing strengths instead of presumed weaknesses sometimes pretexting bias.

Flexible work accommodates various circumstances through compressed schedules, telecommuting, leaves and adjusted hours promoting work-life integration and accessibility disproportionately vital to women and people with disabilities.

Representation in marketing, decor, events and amenities reflects diversity as a strength. Inclusive imagery and language foster belonging for all rather than privileging majority demographics.

Grievance systems facilitate open dialogue on sensitive issues through impartial ombudspersons aiming cooperation over punishment. Mediation trains participants constructive conflict resolution.

Compensation reviews address biases underpaying roles dominated by women or people of color. Quantitative analysis reveals gaps while qualitative methods ascertain subjective influences requiring remedy.

Mentorship and sponsorship programs pair staff with senior allies to navigate organizational politicking and systems. This enhances inclusion and advancement opportunities by building relationships risking exclusion for minorities facing biases.

Succession planning broadens to include candidates from diverse backgrounds through unbiased assessments of strengths beyond stereotypical attributes. Targeted development programs further equitable access to leadership.

Supply chain and vendor diversification strengthen commitment through economic investment in minority- and women-owned businesses as suppliers and partners. This increases representation within the extended organizational network and community.

Crowdsourced review sites receive monitoring to address potential disparagement forming around demographics. Reputational issues influence candidate and client perceptions, so proactive remedy maintains inclusion.

Surveys measure experiences and perceptions across demographics to address deficiencies. Focus groups delve into systemic obstacles and subtler issues before attrition negatively impacts diversity levels. Continuous learning guides improvement.

Decor, imagery and facilities reflect inclusion through representation of diverse identities. Privacy accommodates religious or wellbeing needs through optional prayer rooms or lactation spaces.

Resources committed to inclusion correlate positively with professed priorities through budgets, staffing and leadership support. Accountability measures progress beyond annual hiring metrics.

Data analyzes representation and attrition rates to ascertain where barriers persist requiring remedy, such as disproportionate turnover among underrepresented demographics. Trends inform strategic planning.

Community building events like interfaith gatherings, cultural celebrations or networking mixers strengthen connections across differences. These reduce bias risks arising from relations predominantly within identity silos.

Acknowledging holidays and commemorations from diverse religious or cultural heritages fosters belonging for all identities. Inclusive language becomes habitual, conveying respect through both speech and written organizational communications.

Sustained progress depends on continuous improvement efforts recognizing bias as systemic and often unseen even by well-meaning individuals. An equitable culture emerges through persevering cooperation over aspirations alone.

Diversity Metrics and Accountability

Quantitative hiring, retention and promotion data reveal trends requiring investigation. Representation benchmarks signal attrition and advancement patterns affecting underrepresented groups signaling obstacles like biased evaluations or inhospitable culture.

Metrics analyze hiring success through quality of candidates and follow appointments, internships or other preparatory programs. Tracking sources indicates pipelines effecting more equitable recruitment.

Qualitative employee experience surveys supplement quantitative data. They probe inclusion, respect and leadership concerning diversity issues which attrition numbers alone may inadequately explain. Insights guide remediation.

Accountability lives through allocating resources proportionate to diversity's professed significance. Budgets, staffing and executive oversight demonstrate commitment exceeding initiatives to foster sustained evolution.

Dedicated positions like chief diversity officers coordinate efforts enterprise-wide with competence over individual business units which may under resource inclusion. Centralized authority maintains consistency and comprehensive data collection.

Compensation analyses uncover inequities risking attrition, such as consistent underpaying of women or roles dominated by ethnic minorities. Quantitative tools identify gaps, while qualitative methods clarify subjective influences requiring address.

Performance management evaluates bias risks obscuring contributions from diverse talents, through structured, outcomes-based methods rather than subjective attributes prone to preconceptions. Individual development planning balances strengths.

Succession planning broadens talent pools considered for leadership beyond risk-averse tendencies through transparent, verifiable assessments of capabilities regardless demographic attributes. Sponsorship furthers equitable access.

Supplier diversity expands economic investment in minority- and women-owned businesses, increasing representation within organizational networks and communities served or impacted. Tracking spending patterns signals commitment.

Crowdsourced review sites monitor reputation issues which could form around any group and influence candidates or clients. Prompt issue resolution maintains diverse staff perception of fair treatment and opportunity.

benchmarks signal inclusion across leadership, senior management and board director demographics to identify disparities requiring attention. Continuous vetting prevents stagnation.

Retention tracking analyzes attrition causes to address deficiencies, such as disproportionate turnover in underrepresented demographics signaling culture issues meriting remedy before valuable talents conclude change unlikely.

Grievance resolution rates demonstrate impartial systems exist for addressing sensitive issues constructively. Monitoring prevents reoccurrence and diffuses potential hostilities.

Mentorship and sponsorship program participation, funding, and success in advancing protégés indicates their value versus surface-level initiatives prone to deficiencies without oversight.

Leadership prioritization surfaces through budgets, delegation of executive authority, public pronouncements and personal involvement with employee resource groups and stakeholder councils. Sponsorship indicates more than pro forma support.

Training participation, satisfaction surveys and post-course testing ascertain effectiveness beyond attendance counts. Evolving social awareness requires periodic refreshers addressing new issues.

Community partnership spending and internship/trainee hiring from targeted networks expand access for untapped talent pools. Tracking sources maintains focus on growing representation.

Staff surveys probe inclusion experience, belonging, leadership response to concerns and equitable opportunities for growth. Insights validate progress exceeding hiring statistics. Continuous listening guides improvement.

Development program makeup and funding indicates broadening pipelines accessing leadership beyond primarily internal candidates. Equitable access to senior-level sponsors appears.

Public reporting maintains transparency on achievements and deficiencies. Annual disclosure aligns accountability to stated commitments instead of limited compliance metrics. Progress signals change as an ongoing effort, not definitive outcomes subject to backsliding without diligence. Systemic bias resolution requires sustained progress comprehending diversity as integral to competitiveness, not marginal initiatives. Continuous learning guides equitable, inclusive evolution.

Chapter 4

Inclusive Leadership Skills
Effective Communication Styles
****

Inclusive leaders employ styles fostering belonging and participation. They utilize inclusive language conscious of Varied listener sensibilities. Biased, emotionally charged, or culturally insensitive word choices undermine respect.

Active listening skills like maintaining eye contact, reflecting on statements, and withholding judgment encourage disclosure of diverse viewpoints essential for informed decisions. Judgment precludes understanding differing perspectives.

Tone and cadence modulate to convey positive regard irrespective of social identities. Intimidating volume or impatience risks marginalizing some, while pace changes engage varied processing styles.

Summarization and clarifying questions ensure comprehension across cultural contexts where nuances potentially risk miscommunication. Making assumptions invites unintended offenses; respect demands conscious effort over presumption.

Accessibility accommodates variations in preferred channels, from videoconferences allowing participation elsewhere to open-door policies. No one size suits communication needs universally, requiring adaptation.

COMMUNICATION

Inquiry solicits participant comfort and preferences to improve conversations on sensitive themes. Assumptions about appropriateness often derive from majority experiences alone.

Acknowledging limitations, fallibility and capacity for growth models humility essential for respect. Claiming perfection precludes evolution and bars repairing affinity ruptures from inevitable missteps.

Stories and examples depicting diversity as strengths inspire by motivating emulation. Rather than technical brevity, narratives foster emotive identification across backgrounds.

Paraphrasing conveys validation and understanding beyond cursory responses. It ensures complex ideas cohere across cultural filters which could impede full comprehension otherwise.

Nonverbal affect mirrors engagement respectfully. Expressive attending promotes psychologically safe disclosure from quieter cultures where direct eye contact may intimidate. Body language must complement rather than contradict speech.

Confrontation maintains respect, targeting issues rather than personalities. Impartial moderation resolves disputes cooperatively without threats undermining future collaborative efforts.

Accountability alleviates resentment and motivates behavioral adjustment when deficiencies surface. But punitive approaches sustain resentments obviating atonement and reform. Restorative practices best maintain relationships.

Dialogue establishes mutual understanding as the goal over persuasion which threatens sincerity. Exploring multiple viewpoints expands perspectives rather than seeking premature consensus risking superficial compliance.

Inspiring visionary narration excites collaborative endeavors through inclusive imagery depicting diversity as strength. Aspirational descriptions motivate diverse staff toward shared purposes.

Positive reinforcement rewards inclusion efforts sincerely. General praise risks meaninglessness while specific acknowledgments nurture replicable behaviors through emotional and social endorsements. Evaluation focuses on development.

Self-disclosure from leadership mitigates perceptions of distance through humanizing transparency. However, oversharing risks distracting from organizational missions or appearing unprofessional.

Accessibility accepts participation from all levels and functions to seed inclusion from the bottom-up as cultural expectation. Approachability supersedes authority and cultivates empathy.

Informality tempers rigid formality which could alienate some personalities and cultures. But relaxed environments risk disruptions unless paired with respect and direction maintaining professional standards.

Equity elevates consistently marginalized voices through proactive inclusion techniques from town halls to anonymous comment boxes. Passively waiting risks perpetuating status quos of exclusion.

Constructive conflict serves as a catalyst for progress and builds resilient cooperation. Leaders mediate tensions productively, focusing resolution on shared interests rather than positional escalation which fractures relationships.

Continuous evaluation and improvement sustain relevance through changing demographic realities. Effective communication constitutes an ongoing effort exceeding isolated initiatives in service of inclusiveness as a strategic advantage.

Active Listening and Understanding Others

Attentiveness signals value through engaged focusing instead of divided attention which conveys disregard. Eye contact, nods and vocal acknowledgments reinforce solidarity with speakers.

Reflective statements and clarifying queries promote comprehension beyond superficial responses. Misunderstandings obstruct cooperation if left unresolved. Understanding motivates rather than judging.

Suspending assumptions grants others autonomy, defining themselves beyond preconceptions. Respect demands seeing diversity as enrichment rather than limitation requiring remedy through attempts remediation conversion.

Cultural learning remains ongoing through humility, curiosity and sharing control of dialogic agendas. No one demographic embodies a monolith, so singular expertise provides limited frameworks.

Self-disclosure establishes mutuality and approachability when appropriate. However, oversharing risks distracting from organizational missions or appearing unprofessional. Effective exchange prioritizes others' expression

Paraphrasing restates key points and feelings to validate viewpoints, correcting misunderstandings which undermine future cooperation if left undiscovered. Clarifying Queries Resolves miscommunications.

Summarizing periodically encapsulates discussions for comprehension across cultural filters which may otherwise impede shared understanding. Confirming Consensus builds cohesion.

Patience allows pondering complex issues without pressuring premature replies. Some cultures favor reflection over immediate responses. Respecting rhythms nourishes inclusion.

Visualizing others' perspectives inspires empathy through imaginative exercises rather than judgmental assumptions. Walking in diverse shoes mitigates biases which marginalize reputations and opportunities.

Contextualization seeks relevant backgrounds before conclusions when issues touch identities or histories demanding special considerations. Knowledge Guards against insensitivities.

Compassion acknowledges limitations within discourses involving systemic harms or traumas. Victim-blaming retraumatized while solutions require acknowledging interdependencies beyond simplified analyses.

Confrontation becomes constructive through impartial, restorative methods prioritizing reconciliation over retaliation. Punishment breeds resentment while understanding heals relationships and motivates long-term growth.

Accountability balances addressing legitimate grievances with forgiveness when reconciliation proves possible. Reform outstrips regret if stewardship remains the priority over setbacks.

Disclosure proceeds at an individual pace respecting vulnerabilities. Forcing premature trust risks alienation; patience nurtures unfolding cooperation in due course.

Inspiring visionary narration motivates through inclusive imagery depicting diversity as strength. Shared purposes excite settlements' talents whereas dividends sustain representations. Positive language energizes.

Recognizing systemic factors alongside personal responsibilities prevents victim-blaming but promotes constructive growth. Simplistic analyses impede addressing root causes and rebuilding trust.

Cultural awareness expands beyond surface behaviors to subjective experiences rarely openly shared. Mining depths merits patience and discernment over hasty assumptions.

Bias-awareness acknowledges blind spots within preconceptions skewing perceptions. Open discussion maintains accountability; defensiveness shields problems from remedy.

Affirming individuality balances communalism by validating unique identity expressions. Forcing uniformity threatens belonging for nonconformists whose talents benefit organizations.

Facilitating discussions broadens perspectives beyond initial reactions. Quieter voices feel heard with patience and structures like anonymous feedback. Forced consensus silences dissent.

Introspection identifies tendencies towards over-control or uncertainty which could overwhelm discussion facilitation. Self-awareness mitigates dysfunctions and empowers flexible leadership.

Context appreciates social pressures which inform comments, avoiding absolutist ethics. Circumstances affect behaviors; character emerges from long-term commitment to inclusion.

Empathy replaces assessment through perspective-taking, not just cognitive understanding. Emotional resonance fosters trust were aloof impartiality risks detachment.

Admitting non-expertise on some issues models humility and transfers discussion leadership appropriately. Authority Depends on service, not just status.

Evaluation prioritizes relationships and learning over productive outputs alone. Inclusion cultivates cohesion supporting achievements, not just technical milestones missing interpersonal foundations.

Progress incorporates feedback from diverse monitors ensuring actions match intentions. Standing still risks exclusionary relapse without ongoing refinement.

Managing Difficult Conversations

Preparation establishes understanding of issues, relationships and positional tensions to effectively navigate sensitivity. Reactivity risks escalation while insight tempers interactions.

Ground rules prevent escalation through respectful tone and active listening techniques. Distractions diminish while civility and understanding prevail over victories.

Inquiry elicits multiple viewpoints and narratives to replace assumptions. Partiality precludes resolution; neutral facilitation maintains focus on shared interests.

Acknowledging emotions models vulnerability and normalization and prevents defensiveness. However, outbursts remain respectful and solutions-oriented for constructive outcome.

Summarization periodically confirms shared objects and agreements in emotive discussions prone to drift or talk past one another. Common goals resurface discourse.

Patience allows interests to clarify complex issues avoiding premature answers pressuring resolution. Forcing Consensus Precludes Concerns Emerging.

Reframing redefines problems collaboratively as shared rather than oppositional. Resolution on cooperation not competition.

Compromise supplements win-win solutions through proportional concessions where complete agreement eludes. All parties must feel heard.

Accountability addresses legitimate issues respecting contexts and individuals. Punishment Breeds Resentment; understanding motivates growth.

Evaluating systemic factors individualizes responsibility, preventing deflection or scapegoating. Surface analysis impedes resolution and Trust-building.

Cultural learning remains on going through open-minded humility and exploring assumptions. No culture represents a universal experience.

Recognizing subjective viewpoints mitigates oversimplification. Individual circumstances shape comments to more than intentions alone.

Admitting gaps in cultural competence models growth and transfers leadership to more expert voices when topics demand. Authority depends on service.

Progress demands feedback from parties previously marginalized to sustain intentional transformation beyond momentary concessions. Standing still risks regress.

Leadership facilitates rather than determines outcomes encouraging investment across stakeholders. Forced consensus disempowers while collaboration fortifies trust.

Facilitating perspective-sharing broadens initial analyses through introducing additional viewpoints. No single lens holds objectivity; diversity energizes solutions.

Context appreciation explains behaviors with nuance, avoiding rigidity by acknowledging pressures affecting comments. Outliers emerge from constant evaluation, not fixed traits.

Summarizing confirms growing alignment through reiterating cooperative progress. Rehashing disagreements risks reviving tensions instead of nurturing accrued understandings.

Appreciations bookend discussions by affirming relationships and positive interactions which further coordinating efforts. Criticisms alone bruise bonds essential for resolutions.

Creativity sparks innovative win-win alternatives where entrenched positions foreclose options. Open-mindedness rediscovers shared interests beneath superficial divisions.

Empathy exercises perspective-taking to advocate views not inherently one's own views. Emotional resonance humanizes 'others' and nurtures compromise.

Introspection identifies tendencies disrupting impartial facilitation like controlling urges or withdrawal from emotive topics. Self-awareness tempers dysfunctions.

Bias-consciousness acknowledges preconceptions skewing analyses requiring re-evaluation. Admitting limitations invites correction navigating complex interactions.

Follow-through maintains accountability, building trust. Momentum inspires where defensiveness halts progress. Transparency discloses role-modeling inclusion beyond management.

Discreet after-action discussions incorporate diverse feedback. No single perspective encompasses impacts; variable windows optimize learnings.

Evaluation prioritizes relationships and learning over metric outputs. Cohesion emerges from understanding and cooperation, buttressing later achievements. Inclusion cultivates interpersonal foundations for improvements.

Being an Ally and Advocate

Active listening provides support systems and visibility. Amplifying marginalized voices transfers power dynamics too often silencing contributions.

Questioning prevailing assumptions and cultural biases promotes examination of their impacts. Unconscious privileges remain unnoticed without inspection whereas intersections experience multiplying effects.

Courageous humility acknowledges limitations of singular experiences and openly learns from others. No demographic represents a monolith; differences abound within.

Advocacy protects disproportionately threatened positions through informed, respectful discussions educating without accusation. Understanding motivates reform beyond fear and defensiveness.

Relationship building generates will for inclusion through empathy, not just policies. Bonds overcome suspicions of tokenism where feelings of care and fairness predominate.

Cultural learning remains ongoing with open-mindedness. Individual circumstances shape views beyond surface traits. Understanding replaces rushed judgment.

Educating discretely on subtle interpersonal impacts alerts to unseen burdens like microaggressions draining resources. Intentions differ from impacts requiring adjustment.

Correcting courteously identifies problematic norms for reevaluation when witnesses. Confrontations risk defensiveness while suggestions encourage growth.

Accountability involves others impacted in crafting sensitive; thoughtful responses proportionate to harms. Punishments breed resentment; restoration heals.

Celebrating steps however small motivates through spotlighting improvements. Criticisms demoralize whereas affirmations cultivate willingness for stretching beyond comfort zones.

Perspective-taking exercises advocating views not inherently one's own, building empathy for intersecting views. Emotional resonance humanizes "others".

Encouraging inclusive discussions broadens perspectives beyond initial intuitions. Quieter voices feel respected with structures like anonymous feedback.

Creativity prompts alternative answers to complex issues where entrenched stances preclude options. Open-mindedness rediscovers shared interests beneath divides.

Progress incorporates ongoing feedback from underrepresented groups to sustain transformation, not symbolic actions. Momentum requires follow-through.

Language mindfully conveys inclusion, such as terms respecting identities. Casualisms unknowingly exclude or belittle despite niceness intentions.

Introspection identifies tendencies like controlling urges or withdrawal that could undermine advocacy. Self-awareness tempers natural dysfunctions.

Admitting gaps in representing experiences models openness to correction. No single voice represents all; diversity strengthens allyship.

Resources amplify marginalized networks and leaders, not just monitoring impacts. Empowerment transfers ownership beyond token admissions.

Patience allows concerns full airing without fears of repercussions from majority groups. Forced consensus silences dissenting needs.

Connecting marginalized individuals to supporters maintains momentum. Isolated reforms risk reverting without communities cultivating change.

Transparency shares limitations and commitment to growth beyond perceived perfectionism. Vulnerabilities enrich trusting relationships.

Bias-consciousness acknowledges preconceptions requiring re-evaluation and relearning. Constant critiques strengthen understanding of unintended harms.

Facilitating courageous discussions via perspective-sharing and empathy broadens initial mindsets. Diversity of windows optimizes solutions above static analyses.

Summarizations confirm understanding through reiterations of progress both socially and structurally. Regress risks backsliding by rehashing past problems.

Evaluations prioritize trust-building and learning alongside metrics to cultivate understanding foundations for future achievements. Cohesion sustains improvements above temporary victories.

Allyship remains a process rather than endpoint, as bias rediscovery prompts ongoing humility, advocacy and accountability. Stagnation loses advances wrought through open-minded relationships.

Chapter 5

Leveraging Differences
to Drive Performance
Diverse Teams Outperform Homogenous Groups

****

Diverse perspectives challenge preconceptions unveiling new solutions blind spots of singular viewpoints. Conflict prompting discussion yields innovative revelations.

Representational diversity connects more extensively with varied markets through intuitive grasps of intersecting needs. Insights attract untapped opportunities the same backgrounds overlook.

Cognitive diversity maintains attentiveness avoiding complacency of like-minded echo chambers. Deviating analyses question assumptions spurring re-examination preventing stagnation.

Creative approaches composite varied filters avoiding constrained thought. Approval-seeking conformity inhibits while respectful dissent energizes.

Inclusion better emulates reality than artificial unanimity. Problems precisely defined encapsulate complexity whereas simplification precludes multi-faceted considerations. Understanding outpaces assumptions.

Diverse networks strengthen through interactive cooperation beyond isolating affiliations. Shared purposes unite varied social circles expanding perspectives.

Differing vantage points recognize nuances any position misses promoting sensitivity idealizing none. Balance offsets pulling single-focus extremes.

Effective collaboration fuses contributory talents above positional competitiveness. Celebrating accomplishments boosts morale more than self-interested posturing.

Synergy multiplicatively grows beyond simple sums of individual efforts. Weaving complementary strengths intertwines more than working independently side-by-side.

Appreciating divergences diminishes defensiveness energizing exchanges. Curtailing debate dampens innovation whereas respect encourages out-of-box thinking stretching the status quo.

Inclusiveness models representations strengthening identification whereas exclusionary environments breed disengagement and attrition.

Belongingness motivates maximizing all potentials. When valued, previously overlooked employees shine in new light.

Accessing various problem-solving tools enhances situational adaptations. Flexibility opposes rigidity reacting creatively to disruptions.

Exchanges untangle knots any strand individually knotted. Mutual learning exponentially grows personal expertise refining preconceptions.

Gathering views beyond positional hierarchy taps intrinsic motivations where authority-compliance dynamics stifle. Initiative flourishes with autonomy.

Decision-making gainsaid benefits through diverse testing reducing uncertainty. Broader inputs withstand deeper scrutiny than closeted analysis.

Divergences stimulate re-examining default reasonings catching previously unknown blind spots. Few excel considering all angles alone.

Optimal solutions surface from dialoguing respectfully contrasting inputs rather than winner-takes-all debates. Win-win sees all sides.

Cultural dexterity navigates variances that paralyze cultural rigidity. Understanding differences broadens where sameness narrows.

Inclusiveness builds capacity exceeding limitations of singular worldviews through cooperative learning and challenge. Interdependence exceeds independence.

Accountability strengthens via feedback crossing group boundaries. Insights from "outside" lenses catch gaps in knowledge.

Cohesion emerges from acceptance rather than forced uniformity. Belonging through dignified recognition affirms diversity as assets whereby all feel invested.

Market share capture widens through catering various demographics versus one-size-fits-all. Representation translates wanting visibility into participation and communal problem-solving.

Retaining diverse experts leverages sunk training investments avoiding replacement costs. Appreciation motivates over feeling marginalized and disposable.

Overall performance thus routinely outperforms selective groups suppressing full contributions. Demographics left on the sidelines undermine the potential that inclusion unleashes. Together exceeds apart.

Consider Multiple Perspectives

Curiosity greets divergences as opportunities instead of interruptions. Discomfort with unfamiliar prompts discovery exceeding initial framing.

Patience allows time unpacking positional assumptions beneath surface communications. Reactive judgments neglect contexts while empathy disentangles knotted issues.

Dialogue maintains focus on common interests beneath perceived conflicts. Finding overlap generates synergistic options above winner-takes-all confrontations.

Respectful questions elicit insights into experiences unseen from singular vantage points. Making unfamiliar visible cultivates connection over division.

Challenging preconceptions widens from limited data risking bias. Data alone does not conclusively solve social dilemmas wherein humility remains key. Open dialogue outweighs declarations.

Summarization ensures all viewpoints feel integrated not marginalized. No voice ought to represent all yet together captures complexity.

Realities get lost in abstraction, stories humanize discussions. Narratives tailor understanding particular impacts divergent from personal stations.

Feedback involves continuously checking comprehension to mitigate misinterpretation. Making corrections preserves accuracy over fracturing relationships.

Prioritizing respect over persuasion facilitates courageous conversations. Understanding precedes agreement while debate risks polarization.

Coproduction cultivates collaborative solutions by including varied needs from problem definition through monitoring. No position finalizes answers alone.

Accountability commits elevating overlooked considerations into strategic planning and implementation. Visibility actualizes inclusion.

Individualism preserves uniqueness intrinsic to diversity whereas forced conformity marginalizes valuable contributions. Optimization harnesses differences.

Equality appears differently to people of various backgrounds. Equity means addressing root causes of disparate barriers rather than identical treatment.

Intersectionality recognizes interwoven identities compounding advantages or disadvantages. Categorization simplifies while experience encapsulates dynamic complexity.

Good faith acknowledges diverse truths coexisting minus coercion. Reality exhibits multifaceted with room for ongoing learning through respectful exchange.

Flexibility positively adapts, when necessary, rigidity risks exclusion. Carve Outs accommodate needs invisible from singular vantage points.

Self-reflection continually re-examines assumptions which even best intentions can propagate unintended othering. Growth remains a process over destination.

Consistency maintains through adaptively applying guidelines considerately rather than reacting defensively to change. Principles strengthen with nuanced practice.

Leadership facilitates skillfully, avoiding directing the discussion. Moderation frames understanding while ownership comes from within.

Outcomes improve through inclusively weighing all sides minus score keeping. Valuing cooperative strategizing over being right cultivates shared commitment and durable solutions.

Foster Psychological Safety

Psychological safety describes an environment where people feel confident expressing ideas without judgment. Diverse teams benefit from brave spaces valuing each contribution.

Vulnerability arises through self-disclosure trying new approaches without certitude of outcomes. Risk-taking flourishes with compassion underscoring common goals over personal shortcomings.

Mistakes pave learning when met non-defensively. Positive framing highlights lessons gleaned versus fixing blame. No one has a monopoly on good ideas.

Differences stimulate rather than intimidate in safe settings. Discovery comes from building on others' insights in turn. Synergy grows collaboration rather than competition.

Safety feels supportive not superficial. Authenticity thrives with genuineness whereas image protection hinders. Earned trust emerges from consistency.

Civility maintains discussions on issues rather than degrading persons. Disagreement need not demean while agreement can come from understanding, not compliance.

Active listening conveys care through eye contact, questions, and memorialization—not just waiting to speak. Others' perspectives become internalized rather than rejected.

Validation affirms various representations through acknowledgment without assent. Inclusion cultivates belonging from affirming autonomy rather than forcing uniformity.

Humility underpins safety as none encompasses full reality. Not knowing opens learning; certainty closes growth. Interdependence boosts what individuals cannot master alone.

Consistency aligns words and actions. Integrity means following through on commitments to build reassurance exceeding surface statements. Rapport matters more than being momentarily pleasant.

Responsiveness address concerns constructively rather than reacting defensively. Good faith effort nurtures continued participation and candid feedback.

Clarity around expectations and process minimizes ambiguity as unstable grounds for vulnerability. Structures provide parameters for risk-taking.

Individual agency matters as much as group responsibilities. Ownership emerges from autonomy within clear relational and procedural guidelines for equitable involvement.

Capabilities feel utilized, not stifled, when diversity blossoms. Affirming multiple leadership styles cultivates participation from various personality types.

Compassion counters judgment. People support one another's growth through appreciation alongside advising improvement. Partnership defines dynamics over hierarchy.

Accountability happens reflectively to understand rather than blame. Learning orients resolutions privately while improvements implement publicly.

Conflicts will arise but resolution focuses on restoring relationships and group welfare, not triumphing over others. Reconciliation preserves future collaboration which proves nobler than winning disputes.

Diversity within similarity and similarity within diversity both matter for inclusion. Global citizenship and local identity complement each other when differences unite missions larger than individual preferences.

Intersectional understanding respects how people hold multiple identities which ally or compete. Multidimensional perspective expands recognition beyond selective traits.

Conversation remains open-ended over conclusory. Dialogue cultivates community as process rather than destination with room for ongoing enrichment. Discovery never ends through fresh partnerships.

Progress flourishes through tackling tough subjects not ignoring difficulties. Challenges which undermine inclusion if left unaddressed will fester but solutions emerge cooperatively.

Leaders prioritize relationships and well-being alongside productivity. Joy lightens burdens whereas stress corrodes morale and outcomes. Work feels rewarding service not soulless labor.

Celebrating small wins and acknowledging efforts maintains enthusiasm where frustration could settle. Appreciation kindles vigor for continual improvement.

Flexibility handles changes thoughtfully rather than rigidly. Life presents surprises and so structures adapt while foundations hold.

Lasting achievements emerge from inclusion as means and end. Teamwork magnifies impact beyond status or credits. Common success uplifts everybody's success when people and planet prosper together.

Recognize Contributions of All

Visibility means thoughtfully ensuring everyone witnesses their valued role in joint success. Recognition strengthens inclusion when authentically highlighting diverse achievements.

Metrics notice contributions invisible within traditional frameworks. Impact exceeds numbers; innovation matters more than production. Qualitative evaluation captures variances.

Exposure arises from advocacy, not just objectivity. Allyship works dismantling hidden barriers facing others through courageous support.

Responsibility shares credit instead of claiming sole authorship which reinforces solos over teams. Ownership divides when contributions get aggregated or attributed to optics not substance.

Appreciation affirms inherent worth of work beyond compensation. Fulfillment comes from meaningful service, camaraderie and workplace culture supporting well-being, not just livelihood.

Language embraces diversity when equally valuing multiple styles and backgrounds versus defaulting to exclusionary norms. Inclusion means active effort to broaden framing.

Learning happens communally not individually when groups synergize dispersed strengths. Mentorship flows multi-directionally rather than hierarchy as assisting others fuels our own growth.

Proximity increases collaboration and serendipity. Distributed teams necessitate intentional connection whereas togetherness arises naturally from real interactions in offices enabling relationship-building.

Trust cultivates from consistency more than compliments. Integrity upholds commitments while flexibility handles changes thoughtfully over rigidly adhering to past frameworks.

Appreciation occurs regularly, not just annually or in isolation. Ongoing recognition motivates whereas sporadic rewards diminish morale and effort the rest of the year.

Advancement results from assessing aptitudes, not just tenure. Development prioritizes each person's potential through tailored growth opportunities irrespective of role.

Input feels significant from voting to planning. Participatory decision-making garners commitment exceeding directives.

Well-being matters as much as work. Flexible policies accommodate lives' ebbs and flows outside employment while supporting productivity within.

Humility means learners not experts shape culture. Not knowing opens conversations whereas pretense of completeness closes dialogue.

Diversity itself enhances recognized when inviting various cultures and identities strengthen output beyond political correctness. Differing lives contribute knowledge from which all can draw.

Access provides fairness through equal chances and compensation irrespective of backgrounds. Barriers undermine utilizing diverse reservoirs of skills.

Appreciation regularly lifts morale. Ongoing recognition motivates whereas sporadic rewards diminish efforts the rest of year. People work for praise more than paychecks.

Ergonomics elevate comfort and health as much as performance. Self-care boosts output through accommodating the needs of whole humans rather than cogs in a machine.

Transparency builds trust exceeding secretiveness. Explanations empower whereas uncertainty disengages. Shared understanding clarifies purpose beyond individual tasks.

Growth cultivates potential through learning as valued as production. Development prioritizes each person's contribution through tailored opportunities irrespective of role or title.

Acknowledgment highlights diverse accomplishments, not sole attributes. Wholeness supersedes parts with intersectional understanding of multi-dimensional lives.

Visibility means thoughtfully ensuring all witness valued roles. Representation strengthens inclusion through authentically highlighting varied achievements.

Success storytelling inspires by showcasing varied paths. Shared challenges normalize experiences as opportunities for community.

Accountability operates reflectively to sustain rather than decline relationships and outcomes. Learning orients resolutions privately while improvement implements publicly.

Reinforcement motivates continued effort when acknowledgment feels genuine rather than performative. Appreciation kindles willingness for ongoing progress together. meaningful work uplifts spirits and fuels dreams for greater impact. Commitment to equity sharpens competitive edge through full participation.

Chapter 6

Building an
Inclusive Mindset
****

Understanding One's Own Identities & Blind Spots

Self-awareness underpins inclusion through humility about limitations. Not knowing opens learning while pretense of objectivity risks bias.

Reflection examines assumptions from diverse views. Perspectives derive from backgrounds proceeding opinions. Context shapes us more than we shape context.

Identities emerge from socialization irrespective of choosing. Recognition involves continually contemplating positionalities' subtle impacts lest inherent privileges or prejudices flaw judgment.

Blind spots breed unwittingly where awareness ends. Monitoring reactions and seeking input avoids dismissing others' validity through one's own narrow frame. Discomfort spurs growth more than comfort.

Experience differs from demographic profiles. Stereotyping risks but stories enlighten beyond surface attributes. Commonality found through discovering shared hopes beneath distinctive wrappers.

Listening conveys respect more than waiting to speak. Internalizing others' standpoints broadens horizons away from preconceptions.

Humility underpins safety as none encompasses reality fully. Not knowing opens learning whereas certainty closes growth. Awareness develops through life-long study.

Bias appears subtly yet severely warps dynamics if left unexamined. Ongoing sensitivity training helps notice prejudices' subtle operation below surface. Privilege feels invisible to those holding it yet profound for those lacking it. Advocacy involves understanding positional advantages to support others' flourishing.

Accountability means reflecting on harm rather than blaming others. Resolutions focus on restoration while improvements enact with care for all people. Perfection proves elusive but progress embraces humanity.

Naming blind spots sparks reflection before change. Awareness grows through identifying hidden assumptions and premises beneath surface reactions.

Identity involves intersectionality as people hold numerous social roles simultaneously. Empathy understands a person as fully dimensional beyond singular identifiers.

Experiences differ vastly due to circumstances beyond control. Common ground emerges by empathizing with diversity within shared hopes rather than stressing divisions.

Narratives teach through uniquely human examples. Statistics stimulate but stories transform by illustrating lives' complexity beyond categories. Lessons spark through engaging multidimensionally.

Mistakes made undiscovered remain misteaching's. Learning happens through fallibility acknowledged, not perfection projected. None encompass reality perfectly; growth emerges by striving collaboratively.

Education cultivates ongoingly, not conclusively. Openness to adjusting views honors complexity exceeding surface understanding.

Bias subtly yet profoundly influences actions unless continuously examined. Introspection helps notice prejudices' covert operation below conscious awareness.

Privileges go unnoticed by those holding them yet profoundly felt by those lacking them. Advocacy involves understanding positional advantages to aid others' thriving.

Accountability means betterment through reflection on effects rather than blame of persons. Resolutions center restoring harmed parties while improvements enact with care, concern and open dialogue.

Contextualization frames situations and persons as fully dimensional, not reduced stereotypes. Narratives teach through uniquely humanizing diverse lives' intertwining challenges and dreams.

Experience differs vastly due to circumstances beyond individual control. Common ground emerges through empathizing with diversity within shared hopes rather than emphasizing distinctions.

Humility underlies safety as none encompass reality completely. Not knowing opens learning whereas certainty closes growth. Awareness cultivates through ongoing study.

Naming blind spots sparks reflection before change. Insight grows by identifying hidden assumptions and premises underneath surface reactions.

Stories transform through illustrating lives' complexity exceeding categories. Lessons emerge by engaging multidimensionally with statistical and qualitative data.

Mistakes remain misteaching if left undiscovered. Growth happens through acknowledging fallibility, not projecting perfection. Progress emerges cooperatively by continual striving to see from others' standpoint. Inclusion progresses through humility, empathy, and accountability.

Cultivating Cultural Humility

Cultural humility involves ongoing self-reflection on limitations of one's own cultural perspective. No single narrative defines complex identities and experiences.

Understanding emerges from listening respectfully without presuming knowledge. Inquiries spark insight through empathy, not fact-finding or debate.

Traditions differ vastly due to myriad influences. Discovery happens by seeking common ground authentically rather than focusing on dissimilarities.

Biases form from numerous societal factors beyond control of individuals. awareness grows by acknowledging prejudices subtly held regardless of intent to wonders foster understanding where assumptions previously divided.

Exposure to diversity teaches the validity of various viewpoints. Interactions with receptive listening broaden fractured thinking into whole, dimensional people. Relatability found through connecting as fellow travelers.

Education happens through humility, not declaration of objectivity. Not-knowing opens learning whereas certainty precludes growth.

Cultural influence feels invisible within yet profoundly impacts lives outside familiar frames. Advocacy acknowledges positional advantages to uplift others' flourishing.

Mistakes made unknown remain misteaching. Reflection transforms errors through acknowledged fallibility instead of projected perfectionism.

Contextualization frames situations and persons as fully dimensional, avoiding reduction to isolated attributes. Narratives teach through examples humanizing diverse complexities.

Appreciating multiplicity means engaging various cultural viewpoints respectfully. Wisdoms emerge through synergy beyond singular perspectives. United diversity strengthens more than uniformity divides.

Accountability centers betterment through examining influences rather than blaming individuals. Resolutions restore harmed parties while improvements enact through dialogic problem-solving.

Curiosity prompts questions respectfully seeking other's standpoints, not Assuming one's own view complete. Participation supports inclusion through active listening and support.

Bias subtly impacts all, requiring constant examination beyond surface assumptions. Introspection helps notice covert prejudices' operation beneath conscious awareness.

Privilege remains unseen by those holding yet profoundly felt by those lacking advantage. Understanding emerges from acknowledging positional differences to effectively empower others.

Intersectionality frames identity as incompletely represented by single aspects. Narratives teach through examples showing lives' intertwining complexities exceed categorical separations.

Experience varies vastly due to innumerable influences beyond any person's control. Common ground emerges through empathy for diversity within shared hopes above emphasizing differences.

Humility underlies deepening cultural awareness as none encompass realities fully. Not-knowing invites insights as certainty precludes fresh perspectives. Learning happens through open engagement.

Stories transform by illustrating lives' complexity beyond limited descriptions. Qualitative insights supplement statistics by humanizing multiple dimensions in personal journeys.

Mistakes remain misteaching if undiscovered. Progress happens through acknowledging fallibility instead of projecting flawlessness. Growth emerges cooperatively.

Traditions result from mixing cultural flows over generations. Discovery happens appreciating common aspirations and appreciating variability equally. Understanding emerges through bona fide interest in others' frames.

Curiosity prompts inquiry respectfully seeking others' outlooks rather than assuming one view complete. Participation supports inclusion through active empathy and allyship.

Bias subtly impacts all, necessitating constant introspection beyond surface impressions. Self-awareness helps notice covert prejudices' influence beneath conscious awareness.

Privilege goes unseen by holders yet profoundly felt by those lacking advantage. Advocacy emerges from acknowledging positional variances to uplift all people's potential.

Naming cultural blind spots sparks reflection before positive change. Insight deepens through identifying hidden cultural premises underneath reactions.

Contextualization frames situations and individuals as fully dimensional, avoiding reduction to isolated attributes. Narratives teach through uniquely humanizing diverse complex lives and dreams. Cultivating cultural humility and awareness strengthens understanding across differences.

Adopting an Inquiry Stance

An inquiry stance embraces not-knowing to dismantle assumptions through respectful questioning. Understanding emerges by seeking rather than stating positions.

Curiosity prompts respectful questions exploring others' views authentically, not debating or "telling". Participation supports inclusion through engaged listening open to new insights.

Listening with empathy conveys respect more profoundly than proclamations. Internalizing diverse perspectives broadens horizons away from preconceptions. Shared knowledge grows.

Asking thought-provoking questions and giving candid yet considerate responses fosters mutual learning. Respect replaces rigidity as conversations shape knowledge cooperatively.

No singular outlook encompasses realities' fullness. Remaining teachable positions all as perpetual students. Not-knowing sparks growth while certified views risk closing hearts and minds. Learning interconnects lives.

Humility underlies openness to reassessing stances in light of others' wisdom. None encompass realities perfectly; progress emerges through collaborative striving.

Biases form involuntarily yet harm when unexamined. Introspection prompts examining covert influences' subtle operation beneath surface views. Greater self-understanding grows.

Privilege remains invisible to holders yet profoundly impacts those lacking advantage. Advocacy acknowledges positional variances to effectively empower all people.

Contextualizing issues and persons as multidimensional avoid reduction. Narratives complement statistics through examples humanizing intersectional lives' complexity.

Failing discovered become springboards for betterment through reflection instead of projection. Shared vulnerability strengthens community; interdependence inspires.

An inquiry stance embraces the validity of varied perceptions beyond any single framework. Discovery happens through exchange instead of argument.

Asking thoughtful questions and candid sharing stimulates collective enlightenment. Dialogue shapes growing perspectives as conversations, not contests.

Experience differs vastly due to incalculable influences. Common ground emerges by emphasizing shared dreams above perceived dissimilarities. Connection expands through empathy.

50

Identity involves intersectionality as individuals inhabit varied social roles. Seeing others as fully dimensional opens perspective beyond limited aspects.

Cultural influences feel unseen within yet profoundly impact lives beyond familiar spheres. Self-awareness regarding positional influences strengthens advocacy for all.

Awareness awakens through humility and bringing hidden assumptions into conscious light. Naming "blind spots" sparks reflective change before harmful biases solidify.

Mistakes become lessons through acknowledgement rather than accusation. Accountability means betterment via reflection on influence rather than scapegoating individuals.

Traditions result from integration over generations amid contextual pressures. Discovery happens through interest in variability and common ground equally. Understanding deepens by open engagement.

No single identity defines complex, evolving persons. Respect replaces rigidity as we share experiences authentically yet remain teachable. Diversity strengthens community.

Curiosity prompts inquiry respectfully seeking other perspectives, not debate. Participation supports inclusion through compassionate listening with intent to edify.

Bias subtly, profoundly impacts perceptions irrespective of intent. Constant self-examination helps identify prejudices' unnoticed yet covert operation on beliefs. Humility nourishes wisdom.

Questioning thoughtfully and answering candidly cultivates collective growth. Dialogue shapes deepening perspectives as conversations, not contests, with open-mindedness.

Privilege persists unseen yet profoundly impacts those lacking advantage. Advocacy acknowledges social positioning to empower communities' equitable flourishing.

An inquiry stance sees knowledge as collaborative, not competitive. Remaining teachable positions all as learners. Not-knowing sparks insights whereas certain views risk narrowing thought.

Experience varies vastly through life's complexity. Common ground emerges by acknowledging humanity within diversity. Connection strengthens community through empathy.

Contextualizing multidimensionally avoids oversimplifying lives. Narratives supplement statistics through examples uniquely humanizing intersectional identities and journeys.

Reflection transforms mistakes into lessons through humility instead of defensiveness. Shared vulnerability builds understanding; interdependence inspires collective advancement. An inquiry stance cultivates inclusive awareness through respectful exploration of differences.

Committing to Ongoing Learning

Growth emerges through lifelong commitment to learning from diverse perspectives. No one viewpoint encompasses realities' diversity and complexity.

Remaining teachable positions all as students. Not-knowing sparks insights while certain views risk narrowing thought. Learning interconnects lives for mutual benefit.

Education happens in the community through respectful exchange. Shared knowledge expands beyond any singular framework. Understanding deepens through open engagement.

Experience and influence differ vastly. Common ground emerges by acknowledging humanity within diversity. Connection strengthens through empathy for varied journeys.

Bias unconsciously impacts all; constant introspection helps notice covert prejudices' operation on beliefs. Humility nourishes emerging wisdom grown through relationships.

Commitment to learning requires acknowledging social positioning and openly engaging intersectional identities. Advocacy emerges through understanding life's multidimensional complexities.

Mistakes become opportunities for growth via reflection on influences rather than accusation of individuals. Collaboration transforms errors into lessons strengthening community.

Curiosity cultivates inclusion by respectfully inquiring into others' perspectives, not debating positions. Participation supports belonging through compassionate listening seeking to uplift all.

privilege remains unseen yet profoundly impacts those lacking advantage. Self-awareness regarding positional power strengthens advocacy for equitable flourishing.

Traditions result from integration amid changing contexts over generations. Discovery happens appreciating variability and shared dreams with equal interest. Cultural sensitivity deepens relationships.

An inquiry stance sees knowledge formation as cooperative rather than competitive. Dialogue shapes ever-evolving viewpoints through respectful exchange.

Stories supplement statistics by uniquely humanizing intersectional identities and life complexities. Qualitative insights complement data through examples illuminating shared experiences.

Asking thoughtful questions and providing candid yet considerate responses fosters mutual learning. Interdependence inspires collective advancement through shared vulnerability.

Contextualizing fully acknowledges social, historical and systematic influences on beliefs and situations. Reductionism is avoided through nuanced understanding of multidimensional lives.

No identity defines complex, evolving individuals. Flexibility replaces rigidity as we share authentically yet remain open to revising preconceptions. Diversity strengthens community through recognition of common hopes.

Commitment to ongoing learning requires openness to both giving and receiving feedback. It means being receptive when our biases or gaps in understanding are pointed out, and genuinely examining ourselves in response. We must also make space for candid discussions where discomfort and vulnerable truths can be shared.

This process of learning from constructive criticism or alternative perspectives is not always easy for the ego. But humility and social awareness and the desire to grow as an inclusive ally can help us receive such input with care, empathy and without becoming defensive. We must recognize none of us have arrived at full enlightenment, and be eager to shed limited views in order to see from new vantage points.

Engaging diverse voices may expose our own positions as incomplete. But staying teachable broadens our frame of reference beyond narrow personal experiences. The rewards are insight into intersecting identities and structural influences we did not directly face. It is an ongoing journey of dismantling assumptions and filling cognitive gaps to foster truly empathetic understanding.

When commitment to learning moves us to regularly step outside comfort zones, actively solicit varied stances, and re-shape perceptions in light of new perspectives, we build the cultural competencies needed to strengthen an inclusive society. Our open exchange then enlightens and edifies all participants for the long run.

Cultivating a growth mindset where we see ourselves as perpetual students helps sustain commitment to ongoing learning. It means not believing our work is finished once we've reached a place of greater awareness. Social dynamics are ever-evolving, as are the lens through which we interpret them.

Keeping curiosity alive even in areas where we've previously expanded our knowledge allows us to stay attuned to subtle changes. New research and lived experiences of communities bring new layers of complexity and nuance that require ongoing re-examination of initial understandings. No matter how far we've come, there is always more to learn.

With humility we must recognize our learning will never be complete. Committing to it as a lifelong process means making space in our schedules and priorities for continued education. Seeking out diverse authors, thinkers, and community leaders who can challenge stagnant perspectives. Signing up for related seminars, lectures and skills-development courses.

It also means proactively building relationships where we're exposed to new ways of knowing. Surrounding ourselves with people of varied backgrounds who we're willing to have respectful, open discussions with. Approaching interactions with a willingness to have preconceived notions disputed graciously.

By pledging ongoing cultivation of our social awareness through these deliberate efforts, we honor the dynamic nature of societal issues and identities. And we empower our ability to foster truly inclusive communities that reflect society's ever-evolving complexity.

Chapter 7

Leading Change for
Diversity & Inclusion

Developing a Compelling Vision

An inspiring, inclusive vision motivates purposeful action. Shared hopes for justice and belonging unite diverse stakeholders through common ground.

Vision depicts a realistic yet ambitious future where values manifest fully. It arises from concerns facing communities while staying focused on possibility.

Consulting worldwide illuminates shared aspirations across identities. Understanding socio cultural variations informs catering vision and plans sensitively.

Vision answers stakeholders' immediate interests while inspiring progress beyond present limitations. It alleviates pressing issues transforming rather than through reaction or maintenance.

Clear articulation transforms idealism into actionable mission. Measurable goals and principles promote collegewide buy-in through accountability in tangible steps. Gradual change sustains momentum.

Developing a vision requires researching stakeholder needs and perspectives to ensure all feel represented. Using surveys, focus groups, and community forums allows a diversity of voices to outline current issues and dreams.

It's important to illuminate how structural barriers have historically impacted marginalized communities differently than those privileged by societal norms. Hearing personal stories of challenge and triumph fosters empathy for intersecting identities.

Once key themes emerge, a vision can be collaboratively crafted to address root causes rather than surface problems. Imagining a future where obstacles to inclusion and fairness have been dismantled inspires collective work.

Ongoing consultation validates the vision continues resonating as dynamics change. Revisiting goals keeps them challenging yet realistic. Annual visioning workshops invite new members to contribute insights.

With care and patience, diverse groups can craft shared language bridging differences to focus on mutual hopes. If inconsistencies arise, respectful dialogue brings understanding to refine common ground. No single perspective alone shapes the vision.

To promote widespread buy-in, developing a compelling vision requires strategic communication tailored to various audiences. While diversity is celebrated campus-wide, subgroups each have nuanced priorities.

Administrators require measurable milestones and accountable action steps to ensure legal/financial accountability. Focusing on talent recruitment, retention statistics and campus culture surveys shows commitment's impacts.

Faculty desire curricula integrating inclusion lens and new scholarship opportunities. Highlighting vision-aligned research, coursework revisions and workshops credits professional development.

Staff seek psychologically safe, respectful workplaces empowering all identities. Illustrate revised policies, equitable promotions and mentorship programs recognizing intersectional needs.

Students wish to learn and thrive freely in their authentic selves. Spotlight student groups, support networks, inclusive events and restorative justice demonstrates lived experiences uplifting underserved populations.

Alumni and community partners can advocate passionately with real world application stories. Case studies showing vision in practice via partnerships, internships and post-graduate placements mobilizes broader stakeholder circles.

Targeted yet consistent messaging across groups inspires widespread motivation to collectively achieve an aligned, ambitious yet achievable vision of inclusion.

Developing concrete goals and action steps makes the vision feasible through focused effort over time. Measurable objectives allow progress monitoring, resource allocation and continuous improvement.

Disaggregating qualitative and quantitative targets by deadline, department and initiative facilitates coordination and accountability. Regular reporting of outcomes supports sustained motivation.

Tangible plans may include redesigning physical spaces to embrace all, implementing implicit bias training, diversifying curriculum and faculty, increasing scholarships for underserved students, forming affinity support networks, revising parental leave, and ensuring representation in leadership.

Developing operational metrics assesses processes beyond lagging indicators. Tracking interviewee demographics, recruiting sources, retention rates, promotion times, disciplinary actions, and inclusion climate surveys informs data-driven revisions.

Progress necessitates budgeting adequately and strategically sourcing funding. Partnerships may support initiatives through shared resources or philanthropic donations committed to the vision.

Managing change at its best embraces lessons from successes and failures alike. Continuous improvement keeps the vision dynamic through review of evolving needs and unforeseen barriers encountered along the journey.

Sustaining momentum and buy-in as the vision rolls out long-term relies on transparent communication of wins and slippages to various stakeholder groups. Narratives of change show realities' complexity.

Periodic progress reports distribute outcomes and curriculum revisions transparently campus-wide to cultivate shared ownership. Hearing variations in departmental journeys fosters cross-sector understanding and support.

Storytelling brings the vision to life beyond data by uplifting underrepresented voices and intersectional identities. Qualitative profiles highlight diverse students', faculty's and alumni's contributions, challenges and celebration of incremental gains.

Two-way communication solicits ongoing input for course corrections. Suggestion boxes, town halls and online feedback ensure all feel empowered shaping the vision's evolution. Constructive criticism maintains momentum for growth.

Celebrating milestones through social media highlights role models influencing culture. Award ceremonies, visual campaigns and community forums inspire continued dedication through collaborative achievements.

Setbacks teach equally when handled thoughtfully. Admitting missteps with humility and soliciting wisdom on next steps renews focus on purpose over personhood. Shared vulnerability strengthens community.

Transparency and flexibility sustain long-term commitment through unity's power even amid obstacles. The vision belongs to all.

Strategic Diversity Planning

Strategic planning translates vision into reality through coordinated, resourced action. Assessment informs process improving equity, while inclusion strengthens quality for all stakeholders.

Auditing current state establishes baselines. Equity reports delineate representation gaps quantitatively and qualitatively across roles, policies and experiences to prioritize.

Institutional analysis examines root and structural causes through historical lens. Interviews uncover practices unintentionally excluding while community forums iteratively refine solutions.

Data-driven goals and objectives flow from understandings. Metrics ensure progress against milestones is measurable, manageable and sufficiently funded. Initiatives are sequenced for long-term sustainability.

Planning requires cross-divisional collaboration. Departments each coordinate diversity-advancing efforts to synergize institution-wide change. Advisory boards provide expertise elevating underrepresented voices.

Thorough assessment of the current climate lays the foundation for effective strategic planning. Both quantitative and qualitative methods are needed to fully illuminate strengths and opportunities for growth.

Population-level surveys assess perspectives on inclusion, belongingness, fairness and day-to-day experiences. Disaggregating responses by demographics shows where certain identities face disproportional challenges.

Focus groups provide nuanced understanding of statistical findings. Discussions with underrepresented faculty, students and staff qualitatively explore policy and interpersonal barriers in their own words.

Representation gaps across roles, advancement paths, compensation and leadership are quantified from employee records. Overrepresentation in some areas and underrepresentation elsewhere point to tailored remedies.

Campus climate town halls solicit wisdom from broad stakeholder circles. Hearing advocacy perspectives on historical incidents and present realities grounds planning firmly in community needs.

Auditing policies, spaces, curricula and communications from an equity lens exposes unwelcoming elements requiring reform. Both overt and subtle signs of exclusion inform intentional redesign.

Documenting the current state establishes benchmarks for measuring progress systematically over time. Disaggregated data and qualitative insights guide strategy and resource prioritization.

Strategic planning unites the institution through shared objectives and accountability. Coordinating working groups facilitate cross-departmental collaboration to address intersectional needs.

Representation from students, faculty, staff, alumni and surrounding communities on working groups ensures diverse perspectives shape coordinated initiatives. Regular progress updates cultivate shared ownership.

Convening by role allows focus on positional barriers and opportunities. Forums disaggregated by gender and other identities illuminate nuanced experiences to target.

Annual action plans operationalize long-term goals. Departmental responsibilities are mapped alongside timelines, metrics and budgets. Responsible parties sign off to foster follow-through.

Initiatives span recruiting, support, leadership development, curricular/co-curricular reform, space design and inclusive policies. Piloting small tests change and gathers lessons before large-scale implementation.

Metrics track progress holistically. Quantitative goals facilitate assessment but qualitative measures prevent narrow focus. Periodic climate surveys and success stories capture impacts beyond numbers.

Assessment and revision cycles maintain relevance. Successes are replicated and adapted across units. Setbacks prompt review meetings to refine strategies cooperatively. Data transparency cultivates accountability.

Resourcing strategic plans ensures commitments are backed by necessary support. Budget forecasting projects initiative costs realistically over the timeline.

Funding streams may include reallocating existing funds, expanding alumni giving campaigns earmarked for diversity, partnering with local organizations and businesses, sponsoring community events, and pursuing targeted foundation grants.

Staffing plans outline dedicated roles facilitating programming, outreach and departmental consulting. Search committees strive for representative hiring to reflect communities served.

Professional development allocates funds for specialty conferences, membership in equity-centered associations and external consulting expanding on-the-ground expertise over the long term.

Retention initiatives like mentorship programs, family support services, networking events and growth opportunities incentivize maintaining diverse talent. Out-processing surveys provide exit interview data.

Accountability measures like tied raises, bonuses and assessments motivate stakeholders in securing budget and meeting objectives on schedule. Rewards recognize excellence advancing inclusion comprehensively.

Strategic foresight anticipates emerging needs, budget contingencies and long-term sustainment after initial funding cycles expire to institutionalize commitments.

Evaluation ensures strategic plans strengthen over time through continuous learning. Both progress assessments and stakeholder feedback promote improvement.

Reviewing progress data, climate surveys and lessons from pilot programs allows evaluating strategies' impacts objectively. Over- and under-performing initiatives are acknowledged and refined cooperatively.

Periodic climate surveys capture qualitative shifts in experiences, sense of belonging and representation that quantitative goals alone miss. Disaggregated analysis guides refocusing efforts where most needed.

Focus groups provide depth exploring why strategies succeeded or fell short. Understanding nuances in implementation quality between divisions optimizes approaches for maximum understanding and buy-in.

Stakeholder comments through suggestion boxes, town halls and department meetings surface overlooked barriers or unintended consequences to address proactively. Insights prevent future setbacks.

Documentation of lessons learned preserves institutional knowledge as staff transition. Implementation guides detail revised best practices for orienting new teams long-term.

Networking with peer institutions expands options by observing diverse models' efficacy. External reviews by professional associations add objectivity in planning revisions.

Flexibility and non-defensiveness sustain progress by openly acknowledging where approaches can continuously strengthen. Insight centered progress over pride of authorship.

diversity planning weaves inclusion into the institutional fabric by designing with communities served rather than for them. Iterative assessment and adaptation energize increasingly collaborative work.

While challenging, viewing diversity as superseding isolated initiatives and instead infusing every function transforms higher education's relevance, research excellence and social impact. An equity-centered approach prepares institutions and their stakeholders to thrive amid population changes.

With care, courage and collective effort, strategic planning makes diversity and belonging central to the collegiate experience through realizing an inspiring long-term vision. Sustainability emerges from authentic stakeholder investment at all levels working in solidarity and good faith over generations. Future alumni will then pay such progress forward as leaders in an equitable, just and compassionate society.

Addressing Resistance to Change

Progress faces resistance, as diversity work challenges long-held assumptions. Leaders anticipate pushback respectfully by understanding varied perspectives and addressing root concerns.

Power dynamics shape resistance facing underrepresented stakeholders differently than majority groups. For the former, change signifies safety and justice; for the latter, loss of unequal privilege seeming normal.

Focusing on shared hopes for inclusive excellence overcomes "us vs. them". Dialogue reveals resistance often stems from fears of the unknown rather than values. With care, even staunch dissenters can evolve.

Transparently sharing data behind diversity's benefits to teaching, recruitment and regional partnerships builds rationales beyond emotional appeals. Outcomes demonstrate enhanced quality, not lowered standards.

Leaders model change by integrating inclusion into decision-making graciously. Advisory boards comprised of various identities provide expertise safely airing concerns to inform strategy revisions strengthening communal support.

Understanding perspectives behind resistance allows addressing root concerns compassionately rather than confronting defensively. Fostering open dialogue where all parties listen with empathy and respect minimizes defensiveness escalating conflict.

Questioning assumptions through loving inquiry reveals preconceptions often rooted in incomplete information rather than malice. normalizes growth through non-judgmental sharing of varied experiences and data.

Acknowledging ambiguity and complexity in issues affirms no one is villain nor sole victim. Unity emerges from jointly owning challenges, not blame. Admitting gaps in one's own understanding builds humility helping others do the same.

Testimonials from diverse community members talking personally yet mildly about diversity's role in their development and contributions spreads real-world wisdom minimally threatening status quo notions. Face to face sharing disarms fears of "other".

When disagreements arise, focusing on discovering shared hopes rather than who is "right" maintains good faith. Compromise arises from understanding all sides, not demanding unilateral concessions. All leave empowered to continue respectful discourse.

Resistance often emerges from feelings of loss associated with change rather than the change itself. Addressing psychological safety concerns helps gain willing cooperation.

Conversely imposing change without regard for readiness courts rejection. Gradual revisions provide transitions minimizing disruption while cultivating buy-in. Early adopters guide hesitant parties.

Job transitions support is offered to struggling staff through mentorship, retraining or empathy when necessary, roles evolve. Though difficult, non-punitive alternatives empower dignity for all.

Framing diversity as added rather than lost value reshapes perceived threats. Its synergies rather than trade-offs with academic excellence become clear, buoying willingness to incorporate different perspectives open-mindedly.

Community forums provide spaces voicing worries constructively and crowdsourcing solutions assuaging them. Distributed leadership invites ownership diffusing resistance as allies emerge across environments.

Normalizing mistakes and encouraging second chances amid complex learning curves builds trust. Focus shifts to growth rather than blame. United in higher purpose, even former dissenters contribute freely with time.

Leadership plays a crucial role modelling change gracefully. Willingness to listen and adapt builds confidence diversity enhances mission sustainably.

Admitting fallibility humbles while resolving to strengthen understanding through open feedback. Judgment invites defensiveness while growth begets growth.

Clarifying how diversity directly serves stakeholder interests addresses discomfort arising from perceived disconnects. Strategic connections between diversity, enrollment, philanthropic goals and community partnerships become self-evident.

Celebrating small wins underscores progress, however incremental, towards shared dreams. Showcasing pioneers' courage pioneering fuller inclusion inspires others to join voyage.

Policies institutionalize parity reducing reliance on individual goodwill. Yet compliance stems from internalizing diversity's merits, not adherence alone. Education complements policy by cultivating transformed mindsets.

Periodic climate assessments identify remaining barriers for candid discussion. Continuous improvement cycles sustain steady momentum gaining voluntary participation across environments.

Addressing resistance in policies and formal procedures requires sensitivity to disparate perspectives and power differentials. A collaborative approach works best to gain willing cooperation.

Revisions affecting hiring, evaluations, promotions or budgets understandably raise concerns and should be openly discussed with transparency around purposes, impacts and safeguards. Early and ongoing consultation with stakeholder groups provides reassurance of fair processes.

Incremental piloting allows gathering formative input to strengthen initiatives before broad implementation. For example, diversity statements in hiring procedures could begin in select divisions then expand based on lessons learned with revisions.

Gathering anonymous feedback through surveys and focus groups empowers sharing reservations discreetly to incorporate in further planning. No single narrative should be assumed and dissent should be heard with an open mind.

Compromise emerges from recognizing strengths in differing views rather than demanding unilateral acceptance. Not all concerns warrant policy changes but demonstrating concerns were respectfully understood builds goodwill.

Linking policies to measurable goals establishes accountability while qualitative impacts remain priority. Oversight committees with diverse representation ensure fair, compassionate and continually improving processes to cultivate trust over time.

Addressing resistant mindsets requires patience, empathy and leading by example. Transformational change evolves individuals just as much as systems.

Leaders model growth through humble, life-long learning. Discussions acknowledge biases as human tendencies crossing all identities, not personal faults. Understanding bias neuroscience reassures it can be unlearned.

Safe spaces empower courageous conversations where folks respectfully share mistakes alongside professionals facilitating insightful dialogue. Knowing one is not alone in the journey bolsters will to keep learning.

Storytelling strengthens social bonds across apparent differences. Shared hopes, struggles and complex identities behind statistics emerge through intimate listening sans defensiveness. Common ground surfaces where conflict seemed entrenched.

Celebrating diversity within communities, not just between them, nurtures belonging for all. Distinct cultures and beliefs combining into a harmonious whole, not assimilation, becomes the standard.

Allyship trainings equip willing souls supporting underrepresented peers yet avoiding speaking for them. Together, allies amplify important voices sometimes silenced. Accountability to learn from mistakes maintains progress.

Small gestures like inclusive greetings, name pronunciations or holiday considerations pack disproportionate impact feeling seen in our shared humanity before divisions. Respect breeds respect grassroots up.

Overcoming resistance requires patience, understanding diverse perspectives, transparency in goal-setting, collaborative policy development, compassionate dialogue, consistent modeling of growth and celebration of progress however small. With determination and care, even dissenters can evolve into diversity champions embracing an equitable, high-performing future. institutions where all talent feels motivated to excel. While linear progress eludes complex change, concentrated effort sustained overtime shifts mindsets and structures groundward and organically. As diversity takes root culturally, resistance withers and stakeholders unite behind a vision of inclusive community bringing our society's promise into fuller bloom.

Sustaining Momentum Over Time

Long-term change emerges through consistency rather than fleeting initiatives. Leaders secure buy-in by connecting short-term actions to a compelling long-range vision where diversity and belonging realize their fullest promise.

Incremental achievements accumulate force gradually shifting ingrained cultures. Milestones celebrate progress and reinforce why diversity enhances workplace vibrancy, pedagogy and social impact.

Distributed leadership shares ownership of the vision across divisions. Grassroots committees help address siloed perspectives that thwart cohesion. Collaboration amplifies efforts beyond singular champions' tenure.

Institutionalizing diversity sets expectations that outlive any leader. From hiring and evaluations to strategic plans and facilities, inclusion infuses functions habitually not dependence on passionate individuals.

Iterative assessment informs course corrections before complacency sets in. Climate surveys and program evaluations uncover effectiveness and remaining gaps. Continuous improvement cycles harness lessons perpetually.

Annual action plans connected to long-term goals balance near-term accomplishments with future aspirations. Specific, measurable outcomes address concerns over mission drift while qualitative changes also receive emphasis.

Budgetary commitments to diversity signal enduring priorities beyond transitional moments. Recurring funds support sustainability rather than dependence on volatile grants or good fortunes.

Progress reports share strategies and results transparently across all environments. Celebrations highlight pioneers representing diversity's expanding reach into curriculum, faculty composition and learning experiences.

Storytelling campaigns profile transformative impacts on stakeholders and community partnerships. Bringing hitherto marginalized voices and perspectives to the fore inspires others to follow suit in self and encourage such journeys in others.

Feedback loops gather input on execution effectiveness and emerging needs. No initiatives are set in stone, allowing re-prioritization and mid-course corrections before stagnation takes hold. Flexibility sustains dynamism.

Communities from all quarters play a role in cultural evolution, not just task forces. Grassroots groups organize celebrations, discuss concerns candidly and spread ownership of successes grassroots upwards.

Professional development continuously builds cultural competence within evolving environments. Mandatory trainings raise initial awareness, but optional sessions providing deeper skills cultivate champions.

Mentorship programs pair seasoned leaders with those freshly embracing inclusion to sustain momentum peer-to-peer. Inter-generational relationships strengthen as wisdom passes between cohorts.

Consistent communication reinforces why diversity matters communally. Publications, discussions and interactive activities underscore inclusivity's relevance across teaching, research and public service regardless of role.

Memoranda reiterate support for diversity amid transitions. New students, staff and administrators integrate into a living vision of equitable excellence versus isolated initiatives of past regimes.

Campus-wide conversations hosted by diverse facilitators discussing current events through multicultural lenses galvanize shared learning and social bonding. Dialogue builds cultural agility.

Collaboration across sectors models partnership as the norm. Forging respect between communities formerly divided inspires others to bridge societal gaps similarly with open and active listening.

Periodic climate surveys assess subtle attitudinal shifts beneath surface changes. Qualitative interviews bring nuanced insights that quantitative data can miss for course corrections keeping reforms grounded in real lived experiences.

Intentional successes pave the way for bolder steps. Early adoption by receptive departments and divisions spreads organically as perceived benefits materializes.

Broadening representation in leadership, advisory boards and faculty cohorts diversifies perspectives informing innovation. Underrepresented viewpoints drive new initiatives better serving once marginalized constituencies.

Curricular reforms integrate diversity dynamically across disciplines instead of isolated courses. Pedagogical techniques enliven diverse thought leadership equipping all students transcending artificially constrained ways of knowing.

Equitable resource allocation readjusts previous imbalances with care taken to prevent sudden losses of support. Gradual budget realignment maintains goodwill while building long-denied programs uprightly.

Campus facilities and digital platforms model accessibility and inclusion universally. Sensory considerations, language options, prayer spaces and family services dismantle structural barriers socially just in form and function.

Partnerships transfer learnings between institutions. Collaboration spreads diversity's wins more extensively than any single actor alone, multiplying positive impact regionally and beyond.

Longitudinal studies track multi-year progress to strengthen initiatives empirically. Mixed-methods assessments capture diversity's ripple effects with qualitative depth alongside quantitative indicators.

Celebratory events profile trailblazers periodically, conveying opportunities now accessible due to groundwork lain gradually over generations. Their successes inspire continued investment into diversity's future dividends.

Archiving transformation documents the vision's unfolding as shared history. Storytelling preserves lessons transcending any group for institutional memory benefiting future generations.

Applying learnings elsewhere replicates successes adaptively in new contexts. International exchanges broaden perspectives globally while local applications spread inclusion hyper-locally.

Resourcing evaluation and improvement functions matches investments into initial programming. Assessment sustains dynamism where stagnation risks backsliding. Flexibility endures through challenges and change.

Restorative approaches reconcile residual tensions constructively. Where previous harms occurred, understanding and reconciliation pave the way forward united for higher purposes greater than any past transgressions.

Diversity becomes a springboard to greater heights when united behind a shared destine. Institutionalizing parity sustains momentum by shifting focus from representation quotas alone toward cultivating an equitable, just community for all.

As inclusion takes root culturally, diversity manifests authentically across spaces before quotas or policies prompt action. Equal treatment and opportunity become customary rather than enforced compliance.

Progress emerges gradually through sustained commitment to cultivating understanding between diverse groups historically divided. By addressing root causes which enabled prior inequities, the vision transforms divisions into commonalities between all people.

Small acts of respect breed larger effects over time when multiplied among populations. Where exclusion once felt entrenched, belonging comes naturally through recurrent habits of mindfulness, empathy and care for all members of the community.

Continual assessment and adaptation ensure no group feels left behind as changes unfold. Flexibility Tempers potential disruptions, while accountability ensures evolving needs of all stakeholders stay centrally addressed. No constituency is rendered invisible or vulnerable through reforms.

Staying loyal to principles of equity, diversity and inclusion through both successes and challenges fortifies the vision for generations. With determination, sagacity, the goal of full participation and contribution from all talents lamb or emergent will take form.

Sustaining momentum for diversity, equity and inclusion over the long term requires staunch commitment to an evolving vision that centers the lived experiences and representation of all stakeholders. Through distributed leadership, grassroots involvement, ongoing assessment and adaptation, institutions can embed inclusion into daily operations and shift cultural mindsets. If ongoing professional development, storytelling, collaboration and restorative practices unite a community behind shared hopes rather than past harms, even incremental progress will accumulate into lasting transformation benefiting generations to come.

Upholding principles of fairness, belonging and justice for all through both successes and challenges will culminate in an equitable environment where diversity manifests freely and each person's full contribution enhances society. Sustained, empathetic effort over time can overcome prior divisions and forge an inclusive community promoting human potential without artificial constraints.

Chapter 8

Global Diversity Considerations

International Workforce Trends

Globalization connects economies and workforces across borders as never before. International mobility and virtual collaboration introduce multinational diversity into most industries.

To recruit worldwide talent, employers recognize credentials from varied educational systems. Targeted outreach welcomes experts addressing skills shortages regionally with cultural sensitivity.

Leveraging differences strengthens competitiveness, but also introduces complexity. Varied regulations, languages, holidays and more impact standard operations.

Inclusive policies consider traditions like head coverings, prayer, parental leave exceeding norms or remote working. Accommodating multiple needs bolsters retention wherever staff reside.

Onboarding educates all on navigating cross-cultural interactions respectfully. Familiarizing locals with expat colleagues' adjustments eases integration personally and professionally.

Leadership and workplace cultures adjusting to diversity on a global scale requires open-mindedness on all sides. Longstanding norms transitioning to accommodate various perspectives can feel disruptive if not handled carefully with nuance.

Orientation programs balance welcoming international talent against potential job losses for locals if mishandled. Community buy-in emerges from transparency around economic impacts and equitable treatment of all.

Difference and dispute resolution policies grow judicious handling misunderstandings arising cross-culturally graciously. Mediation prioritizes understanding over accusations in tensions stemming from unawareness, not malice.

Development opportunities familiarize internationals transferring skills across borders with host country's business practices, laws and soft skills for optimal performance. Mentorship eases assimilation personally and professionally.

Multilingual signage, documentation and communication infrastructure welcome various languages within reason of budgets and need. Inclusivity strengthens even with constraints if spirit of accommodation remains.

Host country nationals receive guidance appreciating expatriates' perspectives sensitively without resentment. Exchange broadens worldviews on both sides strengthening skills for diverse clients and markets globally.

Multi-tiered orientation immerses newcomers gradually into host community. Initial cultural overview prepares for adjustments while immersive experiences socializing locally deepen familiarity over time.

Buddying pairs incoming staff with existing sponsors sensitizing to norms proactively. Mutual learning relationships facilitate questions easing integration beyond surface-level knowledge.

HR liaises closely with immigration ensuring legal compliance transparently. Work authorization complexities navigate carefully and respectfully towards mutual understanding when misunderstandings arise.

Structured networking entrees internationals gradually into professional circles. Social introductions provide comfort while cultural mentors offer guided immersion into nuances difficult grasping independently.

Social clubs celebrating various traditions build appreciation for differences. Holiday parties, spiritual discussions and cultural events promote exposure and familiarity amongst diverse cohorts.

Knowledge sharing encouraged reciprocally alleviates cultural blind spots proactively. No group feels the burden to solely educate others; all benefit mutually from each other's perspectives and wisdom.

Adjusting recruitment processes welcomes global candidates responding to local talent pools variably. Borderless hiring optimizes skills availability where shortages exist regionally.

Compensation philosophies balance cost of living between origin and destination geographies fairly. Premiums incentivize relocation considering personal adjustments and careers abandoned.

Dynamic rotation programs share institutional knowledge globally while developing international mindsets amongst mobile staff. Short term assignments scattered strategically prevent brain drain.

Sensitivity embedded throughout HR cycles mitigates bias risks arising from unfamiliarity. Ongoing dialogical training strengthens cultural agility humbly within rapidly evolving cross-border environments.

Inclusivity audits uncover policy gaps marginalizing certain demographics inadvertently. Impact assessments guide multi-year inclusion roadmaps customized for each location's uniqueness and strengths.

Diversity committees activate grassroots participation uniting internationally distributed workforces towards shared goals. Regional councils orchestrate strategies customized for area needs in tandem with global vision.

Periodic climate surveys measure integration qualitatively and quantitatively. Open comment fields prompt candid yet constructive feedback on transitional challenges and success enablers.

Equitable health and wellness benefits consider diverse family structures and medical traditions. Flexible arrangements accommodate care responsibilities transcending specific contexts.

Proactive accommodation reviews identify physical and socio-cultural barriers impeding accessibility or sense of belonging. Budgeting transforms policies gradually with multi-stakeholder deliberation.

Conflict resolution nurtures understanding to remedy tensions arising from unawareness rather than ill-intent. Mediation cultivates wisdom from dissonance if handled constructively through open dialogue.

Learning networks pair staff globally for cultural exchanges strengthening global competencies organically. Peer partnerships foster rapport reducing uncertainties across divides informally.

Leadership development curates' exposure to diverse perspectives preventing insularity. International rotations paired with guided reflection develop nuanced worldviews aptly managing complexity.

Strategy incorporates multi-local insights crowdsourced from geographically distributed operational fronts. Borderless think tanks re-envision operations factoring ground realities holistically.

A commitment to diversity, equity and inclusion necessitates sensitivity to cultural contexts globally. Navigating complexity with empathy, meritocracy and fairness strengthens competitive advantage whilst enriching all constituencies through exposure and mutual understanding. With patience and open communication, policies can adapt appropriately throughout the integration process.

Cultural Intelligence for Global Teams

As workplaces internationalize, team dynamics grow intricate. Leading inclusively across borders requires cultural dexterity far surpassing languages or customs alone.

Cultural intelligence equips individuals discerning social systems and power distance variably perceived. Understanding etiquette and taboos prevents faux pas damaging rapport or perceived competence.

Recognizing each perspective stems from lived experiences and shapes perspective-taking. Reflecting how circumstances uniquely influence views engenders patience through contrasts and conflicts.

Emotionally intelligent peers regulate prejudices cognitively appraising similarities beyond surface differences. Compassion considers policies and traditions formed under dissimilar conditions generations ago.

Virtual synergies demand nuanced communication skills. Tone and phrasing consider how ideas transmit cross-culturally without loss of meaning or respect between diverse cohorts.

Cultural training imparts initial knowledge, yet mastery develops over time through experience navigating intercultural complexity gracefully. Frameworks clarify tendencies more than mandating rigid compliance.

Interaction skills mitigate friction originating not from mal intent, but unfamiliarity. Questions convey open-mindedness whereas accusations entrench positions. Responses emphasize relating, not just responding mechanically.

Self-awareness balances acknowledging norms pragmatically without biases diminishing others' worth. Humility recognizes socialization uniquely shapes each, rather than imaging any culture superior overall.

Nuanced leadership demonstrates respect for variations sensitively. Authority emerges from wisdom and integrity rather than any role or title alone. Influence motivates through mission not manipulation.

Critical thinking evaluates customs objectively without reactionary value judgments. Traditions adapt and traditions remain vital both retain meaning contingent on circumstances. Diversity equips problem-solving creatively when protocols prove inadequate.

Curiosity maintains life-long learning curiosity towards differences viewed as opportunities rather than obstacles. Discovery unveils shared hopes beneath expressions society constructs as oppositional.

Shared understanding develops gradually through experience rather than comprehension. Interactive scenarios equip responding thoughtfully to social nuances more than memorizing facts.

Commitment to inclusion extends beyond tolerating diversity to leveraging it strategically. Distinct approaches and backgrounds fused ingeniously spark innovation exceeding isolated homogeneity.

Proactivity mitigates conflicts originating from ignorance through education. Awareness workshops cultivate sensitivity; cross-cultural mentorship nurtures deep familiarity improving cooperation.

Adaptability maintains effectiveness adjusting flexibly to variances in customs and expectations. Rules bend to broader purpose of mutual success and satisfaction for all groups involved.

Patience endures misunderstandings and tensions as relationships deepen over time. Forcing premature harmony risks superficial unity; restoring dissonance meaningfully strengthens bonds authentically.

Situational leadership discerns appropriate decision-making style case-by-case. Distributed governance shares ownership and builds commitment to decisions most impacted constituencies shape collaboratively.

Nuanced communication selects words sensitively considering diverse comprehension. Impact outweighs intent; a proper interpreter conveys spirit avoiding assumptions demeaning other perspectives.

In a global context, diplomacy becomes paramount in team dynamics. Tact supersedes haste in addressing challenging issues to retain cooperation.

Mediation cultivates win-win resolutions through respectful dialog where parties listen with empathy to comprehend disparate viewpoints fully.

Cultural agility regulates preconceptions cognitively with an open mindset. Complex realities defy overgeneralizations; understanding emerges from firsthand relations not secondhand information.

Humility underpins intercultural synergy. No single approach prevails universally; diverse skills combine to solve problems too intricate for isolation. Commitment to mutuality lifts all.

Developmental feedback considers both content and process sensitively. Guidance prevents lost translation while deepening cultural literacy through two-way learning.

Inclusiveness institutes rotating leadership empowering diverse competencies situationally. Shared burden of responsibilities builds ownership while fostering cultural agility.

Knowledge-sharing crosses borders through mentoring circles. Journals track lessons from transitions maintaining organizational memory respectfully.

Global virtuality presents unique dynamics, as misunderstandings proliferate easily at a distance. Extra efforts foster closeness through casual online interactions.

Relationship-building precedes task-focus to establish rapport critical for remote intercultural cooperation. Socialization includes families and interests, not just work personas.

Creative brainstorming combines varied problem-solving logics beyond conventional boundaries. Divergent analyses spark unforeseen solutions through integrative thinking.

Masterful facilitation surfaces silent voices and steers discussions productively. Inclusiveness respects pace of less assertive cultures whilst progressing tasks.

Compassion counters feelings of isolation or vulnerability from expatriation. Open doors and check-ins bolster morale alongside performance management.

Learning agendas customize training iterating needs. Continuous feedback recalibrates the approach ensuring relevance as contexts evolve globally.

Cultural intelligence sustains synergy across borders through humility, patience and commitment to mutual understanding. Interface management considers socio-emotional elements holistically for interfacing diverse populations skillfully. With experience and mentorship, global competencies accelerate collaboration to new heights.

Compliance with Global Regulations

International expansion stresses legal compliance as jurisdictions diverge in employment statutes. Yet harmonization also emerges as protections strengthen society worldwide.

Conscientious research keeps policies synchronizing permissions globally. Data privacy, pay equity and inclusion guide strategic planning proactively ahead of enforcement.

Centralized tracking cross-references regulations periodically. Regional advisors flag alterations impacting operations. Impact assessments propose compliant solutions cost-effectively.

Training modules educate locally on evolving standards succinctly. Focused FAQs clarify nuances deterring inadvertent nonconformance through understanding rather than fear of punishment.

Whistleblowing policies and investigations uphold integrity systematically. Protection motivates reporting issues constructively to strengthen compliance culture jointly with legal counsel.

Regional HR coordinates regional practices under centralized standards. Localization contextualizes holistic strategies respecting cultural values. Consistent guidelines strengthen reputations across markets.

Duty of care policies safeguard staff globetrotting or posted abroad. Health benefits consider locations' variances proactively. Pre-departure orientations clarify support for wellness, relocation and repatriation.

Compensation benchmarking maintains internal equity externally. Cost-of-living adjustments prevent disproportionate impacts on welfare. Transparent criteria apply fairly irrespective of nationality or role.

Succession planning mitigates business risks from legislative surprises. Dynamic sourcing maps talent availability factoring regulations. Mobility and contingency budgets facilitate seamless transitions when disruptions occur.

Government affairs functions liaise constructively with policymakers. Discussions spotlight best practices for informed decision-making to raise standards responsibly without undue constraints.

Automated workflows track approval cycles centrally. Controls ensure leisure and leave entitlements comply in each affected country automatically. Real-time dashboards monitor updates and exceptions.

Documentation management retains records securely per local retention schedules. Access protocols respect data sovereignty and privacy across regions.

Complaint resolution prioritizes preserving employment relationships. Mediation explores remedying concerns internally where possible before escalating legally.

Employment branding campaigns showcase regulatory knowledge and responsible practices to attract diverse talent worldwide confident in equitable treatment and opportunities.

Intercultural exchanges broaden institutional awareness of intersecting social issues. Representatives collaborate globally on evolving definitions of equity, inclusion and workplace conduct.

Partnerships with multicultural associations advise on nuanced community perspectives. Advisory circles contribute authentic local expertise in policy design strengthening responsiveness and legitimacy.

Third-party audits evaluate programs holistically with law firms specialized internationally. Benchmarking highlights exemplars transferring insights across jurisdictions to lift standards progressively.

Strategy sets long-term goals factoring emerging compliance needs to future-proof operations proactively. Scenario planning prepares for uncertain landscapes remaining competitive lawfully.

Continuous learning sustains regulatory familiarity as rules evolve. Forums share new requirements to anchor understanding behaviorally, not just as abstract policies.

Compliance champions network local managers, staying abreast of socioeconomic conditions shaping implementation needs. Grassroots intelligence informs timely modifications maintaining best practices.

Accessible guidance simplifies complex obligations for varied roles globally. Multilingual, multi-format resources tailor information to diverse user needs proactively. Visual dashboards supplement text for intuitive oversight.

Proactive risk management prevents issues arising from unawareness of jurisdictional overlaps. Regional reviews identify compliance gaps to address concertedly before exposure.

Internal communications benchmark performance transparently whilst preserving privacy. Success stories transfer learnings cross-regionally when customized localizations succeed due to collaborative efforts.

Accountability reinforces conduct through objective criteria applying fairly to all. Equity building trust underpins voluntarily following spirit and letter of rules consistently in letter and spirit.

Management leadership vocalizes compliance as core value creating psychologically safe environments. Open doors encourage clarifying uncertainties proactively and correcting issues constructively.

Continuous assessment improves compliance culture dynamically. Climate surveys explore employee perceptions qualitatively, flagging pressures complicating conformance.

Focus groups dissect root causes of disconnects between policy and practice, involving varied levels in collaborative redesign. User-centricity strengthens buy-in and efficacy.

Third-party validations supplement self-assessments. External audits provide unbiased perspectives benchmarking holistically against norms. Reporting balances transparency and discretion.

Remediation plans systematically address material issues to restore robust controls. Commitment tracking delivers targeted solutions sustainably through owned accountability.

Compliance integration evaluates M&A targets comprehensively before transactions. Due diligence examines hidden risks from cultural or systems mismatches demanding pre-integration preparations.

Coaching cultivates responsibility diffusion through the ranks. Targeted development equips emerging managers sensitizing workgroups and modeling right behaviors decisively in their spheres of influence.

A global mindset maintains adaptability amid dynamic regulatory landscapes. Proactive stakeholder engagement and continuous improvement embed compliance internally as a driver of excellence, mitigating risks from unawareness, strengthening sustainability as public expectations evolve. Automation and skilling optimize efforts over the long term.

Leveraging Regional Differences Globally

Harmonized strategy localizes tactically considering cultural nuances. Holistic value propositions resonate authentically through regional lens.

Market research discerns unmet needs amid similarities and variances. Niche targeting tests customized propositions quantitatively. Qualitative depths explore motivators beyond demographics.

Agile operations adjust nimbly according to fluctuating landscapes. Adaptability strengthens resilience against disruption leveraging regional specialists.

Innovation draws from diverse problem-solving logic. Cross-pollination combines insights globally through integrated project teams. Synergies fuel groundbreaking solutions.

Partners embed multinational brands locally through authorized distributors. Mutual understanding builds community through charitable initiatives. Goodwill elevates reputation and retention.

Local media contextualizes promotions sensitively. Traditional and digital channels optimize visibility factoring preferences. Consistency strengthens associations with quality internationally.

Dual-headquarter models position regional experts strategically. Matrix structures level perspectives beneath centralized vision and values. Representation nurtures psychological safety for dispersed stakeholders.

Global citizen exchanges transfer competencies bilaterally. Sabbaticals immerse personnel in distinct markets to grasp nuances from the inside. Cross-mentoring multiplies learnings dispersed.

Multi-shore resourcing balances costs and talent proximate to end users. Nearshoring complements offshore advantages like low costs with agility. Hybridity optimizes resources and relationships.

On-ground management stabilizes remote operations. Regional boards contextualize guidance for local responsiveness protecting brand reputation. Neighborhood touches retain customers.

Community outreach programs address pressing social and environmental issues through collaborative solutions. Volunteering inspires pride and purpose while strengthening networks integral to sustainability.

Competitions surface local innovations accessible globally. Crowdsourcing democratizes input championing grassroots ideas amplifying diversity of perspectives regionally.

Immersive cultural curriculum deepens staff understanding authentically. Language classes build rapport. Cultural assimilation pairs nurture long-term adjustment personally and professionally for expatriates and their families.

Job rotations broaden career paths globally with regional experiences. Developmental assignments optimize talent retention and agility internationally through enriched perspective.

Localized total rewards recognize higher costs of living proportionately. Holistic wellness programs consider physical and mental health priorities in diverse environs. Tailored benefits maintain competitiveness regionally.

Customizable work arrangements respect work-life balance preferences. Flexible hours, remote work and parenting support attract multi-generational talent valuing flexibility and alignment with personal priorities.

Diversity networks foster belonging through regional affiliation. Resource groups celebrating various identities collaborate globally on programs promoting understanding, recruitment and advocacy.

Systematic inclusion ensures equitable representation and voice. Unbiased evaluations, promotions and governance strengthen commitment through procedural fairness reflective of varied communities served.

Accessible intranet portals translate organizational updates. Multilingual, multimedia communications strengthen engagement across borders through multiple access points.

Regional hubs concentrate expertise while retaining synergies. Clustered offices deepen institutional knowledge of circumstantial factors like trade compliance, geopolitical nuances and vendor ecosystems.

Innovation centers pioneer locally scalable solutions. Radical collaborations harness grassroots creativity blended with multinational R&D to raise standards through hybrid thinking.

Social impact investing applies niche capabilities for public benefit. Cause-related marketing spotlights progress on pressing global challenges utilizing regional specialties. Philanthropy strengthens goodwill.

Hyperlocal procurement multiplies community linkages. Strategic sourcing prioritizes indigenous SME partnerships to stimulate regional circular economies and job creation down shared supply chains.

Thought leadership conferences share learnings globally. Asynchronous summits broaden perspectives beyond geographic borders through asynchronously accessible seminars, research and panel discussions on specialty themes.

Customs harmonization streamlines international logistics. Regulatory guiding simplifies compliance utilizing regional customs experts and automated free-trade documentation tools. Operational agility surmounts barriers to cross-border operations.

Ethical audit trails trace origins transparently. Supplier engagement programs institute stringent social and environmental criteria enhancing sustainability standards regionally throughout the value chain.

Diversified talent pipelines attract niche skills worldwide. Targeted scholarships and internships cultivate aptitudes integral to emerging regional opportunities proactively.

Specialized exchange programs place staff globally to strengthen cross-cultural dexterity. Sabbaticals encourage holistic enrichment through immersive international assignments.

Mentorship circulates expertise through professional networks. Peer-learning multiplies impact regionally utilizing regional expertise in open-access knowledge repositories.

Diverse supplier development nourishes niche ecosystems. Incubation acceleration and preferential procurement strengthens socioeconomic mobility and community resilience locally.

Localized branding resonates authentically with subcultures. Contextual marketing optimizes visibility through regional identities, traditions and passions integral to unique value propositions.

Grassroots diplomacy strengthens international relations. Chambers of commerce facilitate introductory cross-border partnerships amplifying mutual understanding between regions. Cooperative trade introduces complementary capabilities globally.

Strategic regionalism optimizes the integration of diversity worldwide. Adaptive localization multiplies inclusion, impact and opportunities leveraging intricate cultural nuances. Holistic stakeholder commitment nurtures resilient, virtuous cycles of prosperity through interconnected diversity and shared purpose across borders.

Chapter 9

Diversity, Ethics
and Social Responsibility

Fair Treatment of All Individuals

Dignified conduct upholds human rights and social justice. Equitable treatment preserves inclusion irrespective of personal attributes. Unbiased practices safeguard intrinsic worth.

Anti-discrimination policies prohibit inequities in hiring, development and retention. Streamlined reporting assures remediation with support resources. Protective measures motivate belonging through neutrality and compassion.

Accommodations empower participation through specialized provisions. Flexibility recognizes uncontrollable factors should not bar opportunities or wellbeing. Sensitivity builds understanding proactively.

Standardized reviews evaluate performance objectively. Calibration sessions mitigate bias through collaborative moderation. Anonymity consolidates apps just on merit unattributed to demographics.

Pay auditing verifies compensation aligns duties globally. Market-value assessments sustain internal equity with transparency. Competencies rather than attributes determine worth longitudinally for longevity.

Holistic health plans encompass physical, social and emotional dimensions. Tailored resources consider diverse needs with parity of esteem and confidential support.

Ergonomic assessments preclude preventable injuries from repetitive motions or improper environments. Accommodations Facilitate Contributions According to abilities through reasonable adjustability.

Life circumstances policies balance loyalties flexibly. Leave allowances recognize varied obligations compassionately without undue hardship. Balance respects diverse wellness beyond tasks.

Belonging cultivates intimate motivation and courage. Affinity Groups Collaborate on inclusion initiatives through representation. Mentorship nourishes development regardless of persona.

Exposure mitigates discomfort from unfamiliarity. Cultural immersions nurture authentic connecting across differences. Exposure debias through understanding strengths in plurality.

Open-door leadership champions dignity for all. Advocacy safeguards empowerment proactively addressing subtle hindrances systemically with remedy and prevention. Inclusiveness strengthens integrity.

Unconscious bias training strengthens self-awareness. Workshops explore subtle influences harming fair treatment to correct objectively through education. Perspective-taking cultivates empathy.

Recruiting networks optimize accessibility for underrepresented groups. Strategic partnerships introduce opportunities reaching diverse talent pools proactively. Representation enriches problem-solving.

Skills-based evaluations evaluate potentials quantitatively. Competency frameworks assess capabilities neutrally beyond attributes for roles. Customizable pathways optimize mastery and mobility.

Succession planning promotes advancement considering capabilities. Developmental assignments nurture leadership reflective of supported communities. Aspirational roles inspire through examples.

Community investment addresses urgent priorities through collaboration. Cause-related volunteering strengthens understanding and addressing needs locally. Social value realizes human potential.

Global exchange programs broaden horizons internationally. Cultural exchanges instill humility and appreciation of variances through immersion. Borderless mindsets spur innovation.

Sensitivity guidelines establish respectful conduct universally. Inclusive language trainings clarify impactful terminology to avoid offense through ongoing education. Diversity awareness minimizes invalidating experiences.

Bias incident procedures assure neutral handling of perceived unfairness. Anti-harassment policies coupled with supportive reporting structures and remedy create psychologically safe environments for all. Fairness is demonstrated through consistent and transparent due process.

Holistic wellness resources consider diverse needs compassionately. Peer support groups affirm belonging through representation and confidential assistance. Resource Persons provide guidance sensitively on work-life integration.

Accessibility audits enable full participation for individuals with disabilities. Accommodating physical environments, communication methods and technologies remove unwarranted barriers to contribution, career progression and self-actualization.

Multi-faith areas accommodate spiritual reflection. Inclusiveness respects diverse beliefs without favoritism through dedicated, neutral facilities for prayer or meditation.

Bystander intervention training strengthens solidarity. Allyship skills equip all individuals to challenge inappropriate conduct supportively and de-escalate tensions through caring, impartial defense of dignity.

Diverse supplier programs cultivate inclusive ecosystems. Preferential procurement and incubation stimulate socioeconomic mobility and community resilience through equitable partnership.

Customers and clients from all walks of life feel respected. Accessibility considerations and non-discriminatory treatment nurture lasting relationships reflective of society.

Multi-lingual communications optimize comprehension. Equitable access to essential information empowers participation regardless of language or ability level through translation and assistive formats.

Demographic monitoring evaluates representation longitudinally. Benchmarking against labor pools identifies blind spots for outreach ensuring fairness, opportunity and satisfaction across dimensions over time.

Continuous improvement solicits anonymous feedback. Climate surveys examine experiences for themes to remedy systemic hindrances proactively through an equity lens. Belonging strengthens productivity.

Fair treatment upholds human dignity and optimizes diversity of thought. Inclusiveness enriches problem-solving, well-being and social impact through equitable opportunity, representation and support for all. Unbiased practices coupled with accommodation and understanding cultivate belonging to realize full potential wherever situated.

Speaking Out Against Injustice

Courageous advocacy counteracts prejudice with empathy. Allies validate underrepresented voices incrementally influencing favorably through respectable dissent. Unity strengthens equality.

Whistle blowing policies assure protected disclosure and investigation of issues. Anonymous hotlines and ombudspersons remedy concerns confidentially with due process. Accountability bolsters integrity.

Anti-retaliation measures safeguard disclosure. Support resources assist all party's fairyland expediently. Deterrents against reprisal reinforce psychological safety for raising sensitive matters constructively.

Diversity councils centralized grievance redress respecting privacy. Elected representatives collaborate with leadership transparently addressing perceptual biases. Inclusiveness motivates through ownership and impact.

Open dialogue illuminates' perspectives humbly. Exposure challenges comfort zones benevolently increasing cultural competency with resonance overreaction. Understanding dismantles prejudices subtly.

Allyship training strengthens skills to respectfully challenge biases. Workshops explore advocating for others while avoiding privilege and creating division. Intersectionality fosters multi-dimensional support networks.

Sensitivity guidelines establish parameters for respectful objection. Inclusive language clarifies impactful expression to prevent offense or escalation through thoughtful education.

Community investment addresses root causes through collaboration. Outreach coupled with volunteering strengthens solidarity holistically dismantling systemic barriers with grassroots insight.

Global exchange programs broaden exposures internationally. Immersive cultural experiences instill humility and appreciation of variances empowering courageous but prudent reform on returning.

Leadership tone sets an example reinforcing values with integrity. Consistent Modeling Of equity, empathy and conviction inspires stepping forward collectively when witnessing wrong when needed most.

Anonymous comment channels provide confidential feedback. Suggestion boxes and digital surveys capture diverse perspectives on subtle hindrances without retribution. Insight drives improvement.

Bias incident response teams ensure prompt, neutral handling of offenses. Advocates offer support while thorough, consistent investigations validate claims or remedy misunderstandings fairly. Resolution alleviates anxiety.

Whistleblowing hotlines operate independently 24/7. Multilingual access coupled with legal protections for disclosers removes barriers to sensitive disclosures. Transparency regulates conduct respectfully.

Anti-retaliation policies couple formal deterrents with informal conciliation. Mediation finds agreeable resolutions satisfying all parties to cool tensions and repair relationships internally first when possible.

Diversity councils oversee equity initiatives. Elected representatives advise leadership collaboratively on intersectional priorities through open-door participation. Influence strengthens commitment.

Allyship networks strengthen solidarity. Peer support equips all individuals to challenge prejudices constructively and de-escalate tensions through caring, impartial defense of dignity when needed most. Courage inspires courage.

Sensitivity consultations ensure respectful language. One-on-one discussions clarify culturally competent terminology respecting individualized backgrounds. Understanding precludes offense.

Inclusive procurement policies consider diverse vendors equitably. Outreach coupled with preferential terms and capacity-building removes barriers to participation and competition throughout the value chain.

Holistic wellness resources accommodate various needs. Counseling, spiritual care, and family support consider complete well-being confidentially with cultural sensitivity. Resilience strengthens fulfillment.

Accommodating workstations facilitates contributions. Ergonomic assessments coupled with adjustable furnishings, technologies and flexible arrangements remove unwarranted obstacles according to needs. Equity optimizes output.

Multi-faith areas respect spiritual reflection. Dedicated, neutral facilities for prayer or meditation throughout premises with inclusive symbolism foster psychological safety for all.

Belonging surveys examine workplace experiences. Climate assessments identify blind spots for remedy through an equity lens ensuring fairness, respect and growth across differences. Engagement follows inclusion.

Community partnerships address systemic barriers. Collaborative initiatives through chambers of commerce and nonprofit alliances remedy constraints hindering prosperity locally. Grassroots reform sustains progress.

Demographic studies evaluate representation. Benchmarking against available labor pools with qualitative interviews identifies inequities requiring outreach and development to maximize diverse perspectives.

Bystander intervention training strengthens solidarity. Role-playing workshops equip individuals to challenge inappropriate conduct supportively, de-escalate tensions, and defend dignity for others when prejudice arises.

Unconscious bias workshops explore subtle influences. Exercises raise self-awareness of personal tendencies skewing decisions to correct objectively through reflection and perspective-taking.

Mentorship cultivates networks, extending opportunities. Sponsorship of underrepresented professionals multiplies impact by example and prepares future leadership reflective of society.

Continuous improvement solicits ongoing feedback. Routine surveys and focus groups examine experiences for themes to remedy and prevent subtle hindrances proactively through an equity lens. Justice nourishes participation.

Speaking truth to power with care and respect dismantles discrimination systemically. Advocacy strengthens representation and fairness through empathy, courageous solidarity and grassroots collaboration. Equitable resolution of issues builds trust while cultivating psychological safety for all voices through accountability and restorative justice.

Community Partnerships and Alliances

Outreach cultivates understanding through cooperation. Strategic relationships introduce mutual understanding proactively exchanging insights and opportunities between diverse spheres. Synergy enriches problem solving.

Nonprofit alliances strengthen communities jointly. Collaborative initiatives couple expertise and resources to remedy shared constraints or develop talents collectively. Symbiotic progress multiplies impact.

Cause marketing campaigns address pressing issues. Public-private initiatives paired with sponsored volunteering leverage capabilities and invest contributions where urgent needs intersect operational priorities. Goodwill realizes human potential.

Advocacy leagues build advocacy networks. Membership associations combine strengths influencing policies and shaping conversations productively on intersecting causes through unification instead of division. Representation motivates reform.

Consultative forums engage varied perspectives. Roundtables including grassroots leaders, subject experts and multiple stakeholders provide feedback iteratively on initiatives through respectful exchange. Inclusiveness improves strategy.

Strategic philanthropy optimizes social value. Needs assessments coupled with strategic grants and capacity-building sponsor initiatives directly addressing priority challenges. Multi-year commitments maximize self-sufficiency.

Employee volunteerism strengthens understanding. Team activities paired with sponsored days of service enlist diverse talents practically addressing local priorities through hands-on engagement. Purpose nourishes partnerships.

Mentorship circles cultivate leadership reflective of communities. Intergenerational sponsorship through professional associations groom future change agents empowering grassroots networks. Representation inspires aspiration.

Advisory councils contribute insider expertise. Elected community representatives advocate iteratively on initiatives through open-door collaboration. Guidance improves relevance and resonance of efforts.

Demographic studies evaluate collective needs holistically. Benchmarking against available resources and labor pools identifies deprivation requiring remedy to strengthen prosperity for all. Insight drives strategy.

Joint taskforces align efforts systematically. Collaborative working groups coordinate complementary capabilities through regular convenings to maximize coverage while streamlining administration. Unity strengthens impact.

Digital platforms share knowledge openly. Online databases coupled with discussion forums pool curated best practices, funding sources, and partnership opportunities through open-access exchange. Transparency cultivates innovation.

Pro bono services contribute specialized expertise. Volunteer consulting, legal, and professional assistance applies capabilities directly for capacity-building. Skill-based donations strengthen self-sufficiency.

Callouts solicit grassroots expertise. Public requests for topic area professionals to join committees or taskforces welcomes unrecognized perspectives through open nomination. Representation bolsters relevance.

Convenings spark fresh partnerships. Recurring conferences and workshops cultivate connections between diverse organizations and stakeholders through topical discussions and networking. Synergy inspires new frontiers.

Demographic monitoring evaluates effectiveness on an ongoing basis. Annual reporting on progress strengthening inclusion and prosperity longitudinally assesses approach and identifies blind spots requiring adjustment. Adaptability sustains impact.

Incubators foster social innovation. Accelerator programs couple seed funding with intensive mentorship to pilot novel initiatives addressing pressing priorities. Support nurtures self-sufficiency.

Impact challenges galvanize solution development. Competitions awarding prizes and grants for most promising new approaches to documented issues spark fresh thinking multi-sector partnerships. Creativity strengthens problem-solving.

Funding coalitions maximize collective giving. Pooled donations from members and matching campaigns amplify individual contributions allocating through consensus for optimized social return. Unity increases scale.

Advocacy days mobilize grassroots voices. Coordinated meetings with policymakers emphasize lived expertise to shape consideration of marginalized stakeholders. Representation motivates empathy.

Forums engage citizens directly. Public discussions and World Cafe style exchanges incorporate varied perspectives on priority issues through respectful ideation. Inclusiveness improves policy.

Progress reporting ensures accountability and learning. Annual impact studies and convenings reassess evolving needs and refinement opportunities through mutual feedback. Transparency sustains trust.

Donor circles cultivate long term investors. Alumni networks of philanthropists committed to equitable progress coordinate major gifts and endowments for sustained support. Continuity maximizes impact.

Cross-sector councils explore systemic linkages. Interdisciplinary working groups with health, education, business and civic spheres identify root causes and holistic remedies through collaboration. Cohesion strengthens communities.

Conference sponsorship highlights expertise. Exhibitions and featured sessions at industry events spread awareness of challenges and grassroots solutions among specialist networks. Visibility inspires emulation.

Advocacy campaigns shape public policy. Research-backed publications and initiatives applying constituent knowledge to proposed legislation and regulations foster equitable considerations. Representation reformulates frameworks.

Job training partnerships strengthen workforce development. Vocational programs coupling mentorship with internships and placement assistance to gradually replace dependency with opportunity. Self-sufficiency sustains prosperity.

Strategic weaving of capabilities through democratic partnerships addresses social and economic inequities systemically. Coordinated community input optimized collective resources to cultivate understanding and empowerment grassroots. Holistic cooperation strengthens solidarity and mobilizes cross-sector progress benefiting everyone through mutual growth and opportunity.

Leading with Purpose and Principles

Visionary leadership champions equity and sustainability purposefully. Role-modeling integrity, empathy and conviction through principled action systematically aligns efforts trans formatively.

Core values framed as rights establish compassionate governance. Enshrining dignity, justice, safety and fulfillment for all constituents in foundational documents prioritizes fairness transparently.

Anti-bias training strengthens cultural competence. Ongoing workshops cultivate humility and awareness of subtle influences to make judiciously informed decisions respecting diversities.

Advisory boards ensure accountability. Elected representative councils advocate needs independently and audit conduct impartially through transparent processes holding strategy accountable.

Whistleblowing policies and protections establish psychological safety. Guaranteeing confidential disclosure avenues and neutral handling of sensitive claims deters impropriety through consequence and rehabilitation over retaliation.

Diversity commissions coordinate equitable initiatives holistically. Elected governing bodies oversee intersectional strategy, conduct climate assessments, advise on intersectional priorities, and ensure methods address root causes removing barriers collaboratively.

Demographic studies benchmark representation authentically. Regular audits compare workforce and leadership composition against available labor pools to identify blind spots requiring outreach and talent development through equity-focused tactics.

Accommodations policies establish flexibility. Formal guidelines coupled with ergonomic assessments and adjustable arrangements ensure needs are met respectfully preventing deterrence or disadvantage pertaining to backgrounds, roles or circumstances.

Multi-faith spaces foster spiritual wellness. Dedicated, neutral facilities for prayer, meditation or reflection throughout premises with inclusive symbolism accommodate various beliefs as a basic requirement for whole-person fulfillment.

Bystander intervention trainings strengthen solidarity. Roleplaying workshops equip individuals to supportively challenge inappropriate behaviors, de-escalate tensions, and defend dignity for all when witnessing prejudice through caring, impartial defense of safety.

Inclusive language is thoughtfully advised. Cultural sensitivity consultations clarify terminology respecting diversity through one-on-one discussions establishing shared understanding to preclude offense or alienation.

Holistic benefits accommodate various needs. Counseling, spiritual care, family support and other resources consider complete wellbeing - including cultural, sexual, gender and other variations - confidentially and sensitively as moral duties.

Scholarship programs address financial barriers. Targeted academic support establishes opportunities for underrepresented yet qualified candidates lacking means through needs-blind grants and mentorship empowering social mobility.

Mentorship circles cultivate future leadership. Sponsorship of rising talent from various backgrounds develops a diverse pool of skilled candidates for increasing responsibility and decision-making influence reflective of constituents served.

Succession plans strengthen continuity of progress. Guidelines formalize commitment to equity, diversity and inclusion as permanent organizational priorities during leadership transitions through accountability and periodic re-assessment of representative hiring, development and advancement.

Unconscious bias seminars explore subtle influences. Exercises raise awareness of personal tendencies skewing decisions through reflective perspective-taking to gradually refine objectivity and establish psychological safety for continual growth.

Grassroots forums solicit direct community input. Public discussions and world cafe-style convenings incorporate varied perspectives on priority issues and initiatives through respectful ideation strengthening relevance and resonance.

Youth enrichment programs invest in future generations. Afterschool, vocational and higher education support develops underprivileged youth talents through mentorship, internships and scholarships nurturing long-term prosperity for all.

Callouts welcome diverse subject experts. Public requests for nomination to advisory committees or project teams values unrecognized perspectives ensuring representation across differences.

Accessibility assessments establish full participation. Ergonomic evaluations and accommodations for varied physical, cognitive and neurological abilities abolish unwarranted barriers to contribution, fulfillment and equity of experience.

Restorative justice practices strengthen rehabilitation. Transformative dialogue and reconciliatory resolutions replace retaliation with understanding and atonement after unintentional harms, establishing willingness and capacity for future improvement.

Partnership networks cultivate advocacy and opportunity. Strategic relationships with peer organizations introduce understanding and coordinate efforts to expand influence, outreach and talent pipelines benefiting all participating groups.

Progress reporting ensures ongoing improvement. Annual impact assessments quantitatively and qualitatively evaluate representation and inclusion metrics, identify remaining obstacles, and solicit equitable remedy recommendations through transparent exposition and accountability.

Appreciation programs reward commitment to principles. Symbolic and monetary recognition of exemplary upholders of dignity, allyship and justice values through nominations and ceremonies strengthens morale and motivates emulation of admirable conduct.

Cultural heritage celebrations foster belongingness. Acknowledging various traditions increases awareness and honor for diversities as assets strengthening community fabric and shared purpose beyond differences.

Prioritizing fairness, representation, dignity and empowerment through principles of compassion establishes welcoming environments maximizing potential. Holistic consideration and removal of unwarranted barriers cultivates understanding and prosperity for all. Continuous learning and improvement sustain equity as an organizational duty benefiting constituents and society enduringly.

Chapter **10**

Sustaining an Inclusive Organization

Succession Planning for Diversity of Thought

Talent development cultivates future leadership reflecting varied lived experiences and identities. Mentorship of promising individuals from underrepresented communities establishes an adaptable succession pipeline.

Shadowing and coaching programs expose prospects to strategic perspectives. Observational internships paired with executive guidance imparts organizational knowledge and sponsorship nurturing competency and motivation.

Rotational roles broaden understanding of intersections. Cross-departmental temporary assignments combining specialized and soft skills strengthen familiarity with challenges faced by various constituents.

Professional networks strengthen resources and support. Associations connecting high-potential talent through conferences and workshops build advocacy, advising one another on obstacles to advancement with solidarity.

Tuition reimbursement addresses financial barriers to continued education. Needs-based subsidies or deferred compensation models funding certifications and degrees recognize merit breaking down disadvantage preventing growth and upward mobility.

Mentorship circles cultivate diverse leadership strengths. Intergenerational sponsor relationships between seasoned professionals and high-potential individuals from underrepresented groups provide career guidance, industry knowledge-sharing, and emotional support to navigate systemic obstacles and foster future representation. Collective wisdom nourishes aspiration.

Demographic studies benchmark pipeline development progress. Regular examinations of succession candidates and executive composition compare against availability and qualifications data to assess adequacy of outreach, identify underserved stakeholder segments, and advise strategy refinement strengthening inclusion and identification of future leaders reflective of constituents. Insight enables adjustment.

Accommodations ensure accessibility of training opportunities. Flexible scheduling, virtual participation options, childcare provisions, and adjusted requirements or formats for neurodivergent candidates prevent deterrents to compensation or growth restricting diversity of qualified applicants. Flexibility enables contribution.

Consultative forums solicit feedback on barriers. Periodic anonymous surveys and discussion groups invite prospective leaders to confidentially share experiences and advise remedy focus areas such as biases, lack of sponsorship, inflexibility, or cultural insufficiency impeding retention and upward mobility of underrepresented identities. Guidance improves resonance.

Advocacy networks strengthen representation. Associations connecting high-potential candidates provide advocacy, advising one another on obstacles to advancement with solidarity and collective action. Unity nourishes aspiration and reform.

Diversity and inclusion training builds cultural competence. Ongoing workshops educating all employees to recognize biases, understand intersectional challenges, and practice allyship establish an empowering environment where all talents feel respected and supported to excel to their fullest potential. Enlightenment enables equity.

Mentorship alumni groups sustain sponsorship continuity. Aligned networks of former mentees and mentors maintain long-term relationships for ongoing career development, community support and a pipeline of future sponsors thus perpetuating the benefits of diverse leadership representation. Endurance maximizes impact.

Unconscious bias mitigation injects objectivity. Exercises raising awareness of subtle influences skewing decisions followed by accountability measures reinforce refinement of fairness and establishment of psychological safety for continual growth and justice. Conscientiousness strengthens integrity.

Accessibility consultants ensure full participation. Trained professional evaluations and recommendations for accommodating various physical, cognitive, emotional and cultural needs at all organizational levels and activities remove unwarranted barriers to contribution, fulfillment and ownership. Inclusion optimizes pluralism.

Affinity networks empower underrepresented identities. Volunteer employee resource groups providing mutual support and advising leadership confidentially on challenges and opportunities strengthen belonging, well-being and empowerment among minority demographics. Solidarity nourishes vision.

Comprehensive benefits respect diverse lives. Tailored health coverage, parental leave, daily prayer accommodations, mental health resources, and other programs meeting varied material and spiritual needs recognize employees as whole beings with intersecting identities and responsibilities. Dignity engenders loyalty.

Trauma-informed leadership prevents re-traumatization. Managers trained to recognize signs of past trauma and adjust approaches sensitively and supportively establish safe, non-triggering environments facilitating healing and fulfillment for all. Compassion cultivates resilience.

Restorative practices rehabilitate rather than punish. Facilitated dialogues and reconciliatory resolutions replacing blame with understanding after unintentional harms build willingness and capacity for improvement through experience and wisdom shared. Redemption strengthens the community.

Grassroots strategy consultations incorporate diverse realities. World café-style convenings authentically representing the identities within the organization and affected stakeholders solicit equitable policy and program consultation. Inclusion optimizes problem-solving.

Holistic reporting ensures multidimensional progress. Quantitative and qualitative impact assessments evaluating metrics including but beyond DEI to spiritual, family and community well-being through intersectional lenses with accountability and remedy recommendation procedures.

Equitable compensation benchmarks salary fairness. Regular audits comparing pay rates against qualifications, responsibilities and local market standards by gender and identity group with remediation for unjustified differences recognizes worth intrinsically. Parity enhances morale.

Skills-based hiring debiases recruitment. Job postings emphasizing transferable talents over selective attributes and screening initial applications anonymously weakens biases promoting selection reflecting community diversity and qualifications objectively. Impartiality optimizes matching.

Budgetary transparency builds organizational trust. Public disclosures of annual expenditures by category and program beneficiary demographic with opportunity for constituent feedback cultivates accountability and shared governance. Transparency inspires investment.

Parental leave policies strengthen work-life integration. Equitable fully-paid time off and remote work affordances meeting varied caregiver responsibilities prevent unfair career sacrifice or choice conflicts that disproportionately impact minoritized groups. Flexibility nourishes fulfillment.

Social media presence increases understanding and opportunity. Organic content authentically representing the intersectional talents within and benchmarks progress strengthens employer branding, resonates with prospective candidates, customers and allies. Visibility fortifies advocacy.

Prioritizing diverse representation, equity of process, and multi-dimensional prosperity through principles of dignity, belonging and justice empowers optimal contribution for all. Continuous enhancement of inclusion sustains an adaptable pipeline reflective of stakeholders served. Holistic compassion nourishes equitable succession as a duty to constituents, community and society.

Synopsis

This book has provided an exploration of key principles for building a just, equitable and socially responsible organization. It is clear that diversity, ethics and social responsibility must be priorities integrated into all aspects of the business from strategy to operations.

Championing equal opportunity, fairness and human dignity requires vigilant self-reflection on biases, transparent accountability, and holistic policies that accommodate the intersecting identities within the workforce. An inclusive culture where all individuals feel respected, supported and able to excel to their fullest potential is one that nurtures loyalty and maximizes the benefits of diversity.

Leaders must role model integrity through principled action and empower subordinates through skills development, sponsorship programs and succession planning that cultivates representation reflective of the community served. Continuous learning, reporting on progress and soliciting input from constituents ensures ongoing improvement addressing both conscious and unconscious forms of discrimination.

Prioritizing multidimensional well-being through benefits, flexible policies and recognition of employees as whole humans engenders resilience and prosperity extending beyond the workplace. Forming strategic community partnerships and spending aimed at underserved groups strengthens social mobility, advocacy networks and a sustainable talent pipeline.

While the journey to equity is ongoing, compassing dignity and justice for all through sound diversity practices establishes trusting relationships, stimulates innovation and optimizes shared success long into the future. Leaders who walk united with stakeholders of all backgrounds fulfilling their potential will guide organizations adaptably into an equitable era. The rewards of an inclusive culture are enduring for people and profits alike.

About the Author

Mustafa A. Nejem is a maritime visionary with a captain's heart and an island soul. In his island home, the sea's love, sailing's legacy, and leadership's flame passed down through generations with pride and glory. He is a skilled navigator of words, charting a course through the vast ocean of knowledge. With his expertise and passion, he guides readers towards prosperous shores, unveiling the secrets of maritime life and business success in concise and captivating prose.

www.ingramcontent.com/pod-product-compliance
Lightning Source LLC
Chambersburg PA
CBHW080850120626
46546CB00008B/2776